America's Sex Culture

America's Sex Culture

Its Impact on Teacher-Student Relationships Today

Ernest J. Zarra, III

2nd Edition

ROWMAN & LITTLEFIELD
Lanham • Boulder • New York • London

Published by Rowman & Littlefield
An imprint of The Rowman & Littlefield Publishing Group, Inc.
4501 Forbes Boulevard, Suite 200, Lanham, Maryland 20706
www.rowman.com

6 Tinworth Street, London SE11 5AL, United Kingdom

British Library Cataloguing in Publication Information Available

Library of Congress Cataloging-in-Publication Data
Names: Zarra, Ernest J., 1955- author.
Title: Americas sex culture : it's impact on teacher-student relationships today / Ernest J. Zarra, III.
Other titles: Teacher-student relationships | Half-title page: America's sex culture
Description: Second edition. | Lanham : Rowman & Littlefield Publishers, [2020] | Communication with Zarra confirms that this is second edition of Teacher-student relationships, 2013. | Includes bibliographical references and index. | Summary: "The current edition analyzes the sex culture of America and the ways this culture impacts schools"—Provided by publisher.
Identifiers: LCCN 2020001689 (print) | LCCN 2020001690 (ebook) | ISBN 9781475852844 (cloth) | ISBN 9781475852851 (paperback) | ISBN 9781475852868 (ebook)
Subjects: LCSH: Child sexual abuse. | Sexually abused teenagers. | Teacher-student relationships.
Classification: LCC HV6570 .Z37 2020 (print) | LCC HV6570 (ebook) | DDC 362.76—dc23
LC record available at https://lccn.loc.gov/2020001689
LC ebook record available at https://lccn.loc.gov/2020001690

I dedicate this book to all of the administrators, teachers, coaches, and parents who demonstrate the solid and wholesome relationships required to lead the next generation—and to the next generation of students whose choice it is to follow and define a legacy of their own.

Contents

Other Works by This Author

Ernest J. Zarra, III has authored eleven books, including the following Rowman & Littlefield titles:

- *Detoxing American Schools: From Social Agency to Academic Urgency Today* (Rowman & Littlefield, 2020).
- *The Age of Teacher Shortages: Reasons, Responsibilities, Reactions* (Rowman & Littlefield, 2019).
- *Assaulted: Violence in Schools and What Needs to Be Done* (Rowman & Littlefield, 2018).
- *The Teacher Exodus: Reversing the Trend and Keeping Teachers in the Classrooms* (Rowman & Littlefield, 2018).
- *The Entitled Generation: Helping Teachers Teach and Reach the Minds and Hearts of Generation Z* (Rowman & Littlefield, 2017).
- *Helping Parents Understand the Minds and Hearts of Generation Z* (Rowman & Littlefield 2017).
- *Common Sense Education: From Common Core to ESSA and Beyond* (Rowman & Littlefield, August 31, 2016).
- *The Wrong Direction for Today's School: The Impact of Common Core on American Education* (Rowman & Littlefield, 2015).
- *Teacher-Student Relationships: Crossing into the Emotional, Physical, and Sexual Realms* (Rowman & Littlefield, 2013).

Figures

Tables

Preface

America's outward expressions of sexuality have grown exponentially in the twenty-first century. The outgrowth of these expressions is that as a nation we are becoming more and more confused about the very thing that is being expressed. There appears a certain set of scales on the eyes of many. In this moral confusion, there exists blindness to common sense and truth.

What was considered vice and backroom practice, just a decade ago, was once hidden from mainstream America. But this has accelerated drastically. What was once hidden has now burst forth into the American psyche and the nation is reeling from the radical change. Right and wrong have been tossed out by elites.

What were once accepted as uncommon, unnatural—and certainly off-limits to children—are now legal in our nation. Add to this elites extolling the virtues of a new nontraditional morality—one in which where anything goes—and sex is not just what people do anymore. In America's sex culture, sex is who people are. It is our national identity.

AMERICA'S SEX CULTURE

In nearly all fifty states, teachers have been arrested and convicted for sexual crimes with students. Society needs to be aware that teachers and students are connecting through shared emotions, spending time with each other in private while forging these emotional bonds. Some are going even farther as they develop and cultivate physical and sexual relationships.

The nation cannot turn a blind eye to this epidemic, for the problems associated with such involvement for America's students project into the future for their relationships and may affect their own families and professions for a very long time.

As author, my own personal awareness of the issues addressed in the book broadened over the course of a decade. I spent time collecting and analyzing data. I have developed quite a following on social media and have dedicated a page just to the issue of teacher-student relationships. Frankly, this issue is no longer a problem for America. Sex cultures are major problems around the world and statistics indicate they are at epidemic proportions.

I trust that the readers understand that the celebration of all that is good and wholesome in our schools is the ultimate aim of my work. This is the ideal I seek. Unfortunately, the contrast of illicit teacher-student relationships within the current explosion of mainstream sex is a necessity in order to pave the way toward movement toward the ideal.

Affecting All Facets of Life

More broadly, the sex culture has touched every facet of life, all manners of business, and our nation's schools. Today's students are more brazen and bold about sex, and so are teachers. More and more teachers are being arrested for sex with students, and they seem to find younger and young victims. Teachers are starring in their own porn films, moonlighting as prostitutes, and wonder why they cannot live one way at work and another at home. Families, schools, athletics, politics, ministry, and even our military have not escaped this decline in morality. Even the average worker with a computer is schooled on the NSFW acronym and has to be careful what is now viewed on work devices.

Children in libraries are becoming more accustomed to being greeted in some cities by drag queens who read the lesbian, gay. bisexual, transgender, and queer (LGBTQ+) stories to children.[1] Aside from the confusion over who we are, the nation is headlong into addictions like never before. Sex addicts are on the rise, due in no small measure to online pornography. Sexual predators are using the Dark Web to communicate and pass around children for sex. Sex trafficking is a horrendous blight in the United States, but it is also a major worldwide problem.[2]

People fall from grace due to sex. Addictions are rampant and the addicts cannot seem to get enough visual stimulation, even with billions of places to go to find pornography online.

Changes in Attitudes and Behaviors

Attitudes and behaviors have changed significantly in the area of sexuality, and behaviors once deemed off-limits are now mainstream. When one considers the sales of the recent *Shades of Grey* series, which amounted to 100 million copies worldwide between 2012 and 2014, pornography had made it into the homes and mainstream theaters around the nation and the world.[3] In the midst of all this sex mania and confusion, there sits America's students.

Students are now more highly sexualized and mentally stimulated by the inputs of sex that it has become a major problem that will eventually affect their adult relationships and lead to divorce.[4] Moreover, one particular area where these attitudes and behaviors have changed dramatically is teacher-student relationships. Students are now as uncertain about their relationships with their teachers as teachers are with their students. They both are unclear as to their own personal identities. It is a confused and terrible state in which to coexist.

America's Sex Culture Confusion

The cultural shift has blurred lines of authority and the result is pursuit of pleasure. Confusion of morals and ethical direction can now more easily turn toward illegal activities. There appears little resistance in education for teachers to groom and nurture intimate physical and sexual relationships between them and students. Many Americans are very upset at the aggressive approach taken by sex advocates to expose and indoctrinate their children. Children should not be sexualized as objects.[5] Our culture is sex-crazy. Teacher-student sexual relationships have not escaped this craze. In fact, the National Education Association assists in perpetuating the confusion.[6]

An example of how diverse and confusing the sex culture has become for the average American over the past decade. The following terms illustrate this confusion within the LGBTQIA+ identities:

- L—Lesbian
- G—Gay
- B—Bisexual[7]
- T—Transsexual/Transgender
- Q—Questioning/Queer
- I—Intersex
- A—Asexual
- Others include: Pansexual, Demisexual, Graysexual, Cisgender, Gender Nonconforming (GNC), Nonbinary, Genderqueer, Gender Fluid, Gender-Neutral, MAAB (Male-assigned at birth), FAAB (Female-assigned at birth), UAAB (Unassigned at birth), Cishet, Gender Questioning, and Gender Transition.

Adding to the confusion are the choices of the numbers of genders that are now available, from which to identify. There are some fifteen options given by social scientists. It was not all that long ago, before psychologists and social scientists decided that biology and birth have nothing to do with sex and gender any longer and that children were simply born as male and female. But now the sex culture has redefined the sex and gender landscape.

People are told that they are not what they are labeled at birth but what they choose to be. Now "because there are more than two genders. Gender is a spectrum, not a binary."[8] These are some of the same psychologists who have formed a taskforce to promote multiple sex partners as a protected class of relationships.

The term the American Psychological Society has decided to assign this class they are seeking protection for is called those in "Consensual Non-Monogamous Relationships (CNM)."[9] These types of relationships include "people who practice polyamory, open relationships, swinging, relationship anarchy, and other types of ethical non-monogamous relationships." What many feared when the doors opened to redefine the norm of traditional monogamy, between a man and a woman, is now coming to pass.

In the twenty-first-century America, it is apparent that anything goes sexually. In fact, the cochair of the committee on adolescent sexuality for the American College of Pediatricians, Dr. Andre Can Mol, predicted that arriving at this point in culture "is the entirely expected and predicted consequence of what happens when ideology replaces science."[10]

The fact is that pronouns are now off-limits, because someone might use a pronoun that is contrary to the way another has identified for the moment. When adults make these choices for themselves, they cannot expect others to comply with their choices and they must not involve children in the web of gender and sexual confusion.[11]

Deliberately confusing children does not sit well with the majority of the nation. Confused children have a lost sense of direction about themselves, where they fit in, and about who and what they are.[12] Predators of mind and body are trolling around seeking to devour the minds and hearts of the next generation.

THE REASONS FOR WRITING THIS BOOK

There are four major reasons why I chose to write this book. *First*, Rowman & Littlefield graciously agreed that editing and rewriting the first edition of my previous book on this topic, *Teacher-Student Relationships: Crossing into the Emotional, Physical, and Sexual Realms*, would be very timely. Given that so much has occurred in schools between teachers and students from the time of the first edition, the time had come to reexamine the issues addressed in both the first edition and those arising subsequent to the release of the first edition.

Our culture has changed and it is affecting schools deeply. More and more teachers are being swept up in choices that are ruining many lives, including their own. Inappropriate behaviors, resulting in scores of teachers being arrested and convicted of sex crimes with students, continue to increase and states are in panic mode over what to do. States need teachers, but there is a national shortage and it does not seem to be ending any time soon. Some states, to their credit, have changed many of their approaches since the first edition was released. This book reflects some of those changes and offers suggestions for states. I also address ways to alleviate teacher shortages in my 2019 Rowman & Littlefield release, *The Age of Teacher Shortages: Reasons, Responsibilities, Reactions.*

Second, over the past decade America has experienced an explosion of *sex gone mainstream* in society. High-profile arrests of child sexual predators, Hollywood moguls, and online child sex traffickers have exposed the horrific underbelly of once-underground perverted subculture into the mainstream of American consciousness. The pulse of the nation's cultural changes has sped up. The understanding of family, marriage, relationships, personal identity, sexual behaviors, sexual orientations and preferences, along with sex scandals that have rocked the nation, are all now part of America's daily dialogue.

Third, the sex culture just described has impacted children and young adults in some very provocative and corruptible ways. Today's children have been sexualized and coupled with the statistic that nearly all middle and high schoolers have smartphones means they have access to the radical sex culture and its messages. These are the messages that shape youthful ideas about sex, and statistics reveal the extent of the proliferation of the messaging.

Sex Comes to Campus

Sex comes to campus in the form of education. Groups that were not allowed to present alternate lifestyles just a few years ago are now given carte blanche to share their ideas and sexual practices right inside America's schoolrooms—sometimes without parents' awareness. Therefore, this book is intended as a tool for parents and teachers, so they are informed about the ways sex ideologies are finding inroads into the minds and memories of children.

There are reasons why students would choose to have an inappropriate relationship with a teacher. The origination of such an idea is now front and center in America's sex culture. There is no secret that the more that children and young adults are exposed to something, the more curious they become about it. In the case of sex, curiosity often turns to temptation.

The *fourth* reason for writing this book is to continue to lobby states and school districts to reform their hiring practices, by changing their interviewing process to reflect the twenty-first-century sex culture. Laws should change and policies should be revised to insure safer environments for teachers and students. Parents now have to worry about sexualizing of their children as yet another form of possible trauma and violence upon their young lives. This book suggests policy changes and brings attention to the reasons for the changes.

IMPORTANCE OF THE ISSUES ADDRESSED

These issues need to be taken seriously. They should be addressed in all colleges, professional-development meetings, faculty meetings, and even town hall and school board meetings. Certainly, all district and school administrator–parent meetings should address these concerns in schools.

Sex education classes are not what they used to be. Today's children are experiencing hands on sex-ed. Girls are taught how to put on condoms, by using bananas. Children are taught about safe anal sex between men, and teachers coming out to their classes is the newest fad. Today's classroom sex exposure is a far cry from basic reproduction videos of the past.

Still, in so many teacher education institutions, many new teachers are not informed as to the nature and characteristics of appropriate and inappropriate relationships with their students. Appropriate teacher-student relationships are addressed in passing, by focusing on what to do and not balanced with what not to do. Not addressing the latter may result in allegations of negligence directed toward schools of education in the near future. As a result of this concern, I recommend this book to fellow university and college professors who train teachers and to those students who might have an interest in education as a profession.

This book should be part of a general studies course on American culture. I also recommend this book to parents and teenagers. Teenagers dialoguing with parents and other trusted stakeholders is a good thing for society. There are many external voices clamoring for the souls of our nation's children. However, what was external has now found a new welcoming residence. America's sex culture is now part of the internal voices of far too many young teachers and their students.

INSPIRATION FOR THE BOOK

This book came about as the result of a four-decade-long career and the personal and professional relationships developed with my colleagues, students, and their families. There is nothing quite like standing in front of thousands of students, over the course of a career, and watching their expressions as I relate my personal story to them.

The opportunities I had to help train teachers at three different colleges for almost two decades are ingrained in my mind and heart. There is nothing like seeing students—the fruits of one's labors—grow into mature professionals with clear boundaries. These are the drivers of inspiration behind much of what I write—including this book!

The reality is that without students there are no teachers. It doesn't work the other way around. Students continue to inspire me to perform better as a professional. They drive me to excel as an educator and as a person. I would not be the person I am, were it not for my loving and supportive family and the excellent colleagues and educational professionals who have surrounded me and helped me along in the profession. I am blessed to have found my life's calling and to be relevant on some level after a lengthy career.

STRUCTURE OF THE BOOK

This book is structured in such a way as to keep the readers engaged. The chapter sequencing is purposeful and flows thematically. The chapters are different from the first edition. The chapters are informative and provocative as well as user-friendly for people on all levels. To this end, each chapter is written so that it may be taken together with other chapters as a whole or as a stand-alone lecture to a class or for a class group activity. To accomplish the latter, summaries are provided at the end of each of the six chapters followed by discussion questions. The questions are provided for professional development purposes, for extending small-group discussions, and for encouraging individual readers to review and apply the material presented.

Chapter 1 focuses on the brains of children, especially teenagers, their maturity and emotions. The chapter describes the development of brains and the impact of neuroscience upon teaching and learning in the classroom. The chapter also includes discussions on emotional intelligence (EI) and the brain differences between genders.

Next, in chapter 2, there is a detailed examination of the choices that come along with temptations in America's sex culture by means of technology. These are weighed in relation to the increased inappropriate teacher-student relationships. Topics such as sexual identity, sexual expression, sexual boldness, sexual fantasy, and the cultural voices affecting relationships are introduced and addressed.

Chapter 3 is an explanation of America's hypersexuality and how this sex culture affects the relationships between teachers and students. The chapter details how sex emerged as mainstream and the proliferation of sex into nearly every facet of American society. Helpful principles are provided for teachers to consider appropriate communication with students and ways to navigate the high-tech but interpersonal aspects of appropriate relationships with students.

Chapter 4 is a specific examination of the nature of teacher-student relationships and the boundaries necessary both in the classroom and outside the classroom. Questions relating to professional and personal proximities are presented for the readers to know the differences. Also provided for the readers are teacher anecdotes and an examination of basic flaws in thinking that lead to poor choices with students. There are helpful tools in this chapter, including tables, which will assist the readers in understanding shared traits of inappropriate teacher-student relationships, as well as some of the conclusions drawn from teachers who have crossed the lines with students.

Schools can do better to train faculty to focus on morality, purpose, and sense of mission, and they can do a better job defining at-school and after-school teacher-student relationships with common sense and confidence.

Chapter 5 is an analysis of the technology and social media platforms used today by teachers and students. The chapter also details the increased risks of teachers sharing online with students, away from school and asks the question for teachers, students, and parents to consider in their relationships: *How close is too close?*

Technology has become a boon to today's sexual predators. Due to the easier access between teachers and students, this chapter provides principles for teachers to follow to make certain that their communications between them and students are appropriate. In addition to these principles, the chapter also includes an online test for teachers to determine whether appropriate boundaries have been established and are being followed.

Chapter 6 is the last chapter in the book and it takes a deeper look into the policies of states and school districts, calling for each of these stakeholders to become more proactive, rather than reactive. The chapter speaks about professional conduct for teachers, the teacher given to immoral living, and a reformed teacher candidate interview process. The interview process is included in this chapter, in terms of both the questions to be asked on written applications and through oral interviews and the rationales for each of the questions.

NOTES

1. Marcus Harrison Green. "King County libraries drag queen story hours engage many and enrage others." *Seattle Times*. June 30, 2019. Retrieved from https://

www.seattletimes.com/seattle-news/drag-queen-story-hours-spark-outpouring-of-support-despite-protests/.

2. Jaclyn Galluci. "Human trafficking is an epidemic in the U.S. It's also a big business." *Fortune*. April 14, 2019. Retrieved from https://fortune.com/2019/04/14/human-sex-trafficking-us-slavery/.

3. Andy Lewis. "'Fifty shades of grey' hit 100 million." *The Hollywood Reporter*. February 26, 2014. Retrieved from https://www.hollywoodreporter.com/news/fifty-shades-grey-sales-hit-683852.

4. Belinda Luscombe. "People more likely to divorce after they start watching porn, study says." *Time*. August 23, 2016. Retrieved from https://time.com/4461451/people-more-likely-to-divorce-after-they-start-watching-porn-says-study/.

5. Laura Fay. "Rethinking sex ed for the #MeToo moment: A 'hugely significant' study shows that strengthening education on relationships & consent can change the culture." *LA School Report*. April 1, 2019. Retrieved from http://laschoolreport.com/rethinking-sex-ed-for-the-metoo-moment-a-hugely-significant-study-shows-that-strengthening-education-on-biology-relationships-consent-can-change-the-culture/.

6. Peter LaBarbera. "Teachers' union radically promotes transgender ideology, Trump-bashing." *Lifesite News*. July 7, 2017. Retrieved from https://www.lifesite news.com/news/teachers-union-radically-promotes-gender-ideology-trump-bashing.

7. Janine Puhak. "Washington married couple, woman open up about 'throuple' relationship, lifestyle." *Fox News*. October 19, 2019. Retrieved from https://www.foxnews.com/lifestyle/washington-throuple-relationship-lifestyle.

8. Samantha McLaren. "15 Gender identity terms you need to know to build an inclusive workplace." *Linked In*. May 20, 2019. Retrieved from https://business.linkedin.com/talent-solutions/blog/diversity/2019/15-gender-identity-terms-for-inclusive-workplace.

9. Susan Berry. "APA task force promotes multiple sex partner status as legally protected class." *Breitbart*. July 11, 2019. Retrieved from https://www.breitbart.com/politics/2019/07/11/apa-task-force-promotes-multiple-sex-partner-status-as-legally-protected-class/.

10. Staff. "Breaking: Judge overturns jury, says father will have a say in whether mother can transition son into a girl." *Christian News*. October 24, 2019. Retrieved from https://christiannews.net/2019/10/24/judge-overturns-jury-says-father-will-have-a-say-in-whether-mother-can-transition-son-into-girl/.

11. Staff. "Breaking: Judge overturns jury, says father will have a say in whether mother can transition son into a girl." *Christian News*. October 24, 2019. Retrieved from https://christiannews.net/2019/10/24/judge-overturns-jury-says-father-will-have-a-say-in-whether-mother-can-transition-son-into-girl/.

12. Staff. "Helping children with gender identity confusion." *Focus on the Family*. 2017. Retrieved from http://media.focusonthefamily.com/topicinfo/helping-children-with-gender-identity-confusion.pdf.

Acknowledgments

When the average teacher sees a problem in education and states an interest in writing a book about it, one or more responses can be expected. Some of these responses include laughter and doubt, various levels of support, envy, and even some professional yawns. Each of these happened upon the mention of the first edition of this book, *Teacher-Student Relationships: Crossing into the Emotional, Physical, and Sexual Realms*. The most motivational response was that of laughter and doubt. There is just something about being told an idea was laughable and that it was not possible to get administrators to listen to what I had to say on a topic.

The first acknowledgment of this second edition goes to the naysaying colleagues. I am indebted for the motivation you provided. Now that some of you are in administration, it is quite interesting that you understand the proactive direction I was headed.

Second, I must acknowledge my former colleagues and students at Lewis-Clark State College. Your encouragement and affirmation were exactly what this project needed. I am pleased to have played a small part in your careers and professions. I count you all as friends and colleagues.

Third, I am grateful to law enforcement. The overwhelming majority are solid and caring professionals. The job you do is amazing and I thank you for your advice and insights into some of the more difficult cases in this book.

Next, on a professional development level, I will never forget the moment I heard back from the publisher for the first edition of this book to be published. I was sitting in an Eric Jensen Seminar on *Brain Research and Instructional Strategies*. His encouragement and eventual endorsement were pivotal for the completion of the project. I now offer professional development on appropriate teacher-students relationships and I am grateful that Eric took the time to acknowledge me.

Last, I have to thank all the contributors to my Facebook Groups, Twitter feeds, and LinkedIn posts. There is a wealth of knowledge that is available in the experiences of real-life teachers, coaches, and administrators. Your contributions to this second edition are so very much appreciated. Also, I am humbled by the teenage students who willingly shared their stories of inappropriate relationships with teachers. Your bravery is honored by this book.

In closing, my prayer is that this book is the catalyst for so many other wonderful and dedicated professionals to learn about students, their brains, and to continue to develop appropriate relationships. I also pray that those harmed in any way by being sexually victimized by someone in education, yet remain quiet about, would be encouraged to step forward. Do as others have done and use this book as your strength to begin the process of healing. Please tell someone and hand them this book or contact me.

I acknowledge that you exist and I understand you.

Chapter 1

Brains, Maturity, and Emotions

*There are gender differences in our emotional system . . . the amygda-
lae . . . small, almond-shaped brain structures . . . located deep in the
temporal lobes at the foot of the hippocampus in each hemisphere . . . they
operate differently in males and females. The male processes emotions in
the right amygdala . . . more globally. It helps . . . understand why those
with male traits . . . often are comfortable with the 'gist' of things for an
explanation of an emotional event . . . The female amygdala processes
emotions in the left hemisphere. This results in memories encoded more in
parts and sequentially. Those with female traits are more likely to want to
unpack an emotional event and process it, often in some detail.*[1]

What happens when children reach puberty earlier and adulthood later? The
answer is: a good deal of teenage weirdness. Fortunately, developmental
psychologists and neuroscientists are starting to explain the foundations of
that weirdness. The crucial new idea is that there are two different neural and
psychological systems that interact to turn children into adults.[2] These functions have their central interactions in the brain.

STUDENTS' BRAINS

Researchers are uncovering more about the physical and chemical workings
in the developing teenage brain in terms of memory transfer and information
storage and retrieval. The latest discoveries about student learning are very
exciting—literally—as they involve the emotional center of the brain. One
of the more recent discoveries is that children, especially teenagers, have
an abundance of synapses—or regions where nerve impulses transmit and
receive.

These synapses emit the *excitement-oriented* neurotransmitter called *glutamate*. Synapses encompass the axon terminal of a neuron, where neurotransmitters, such as glutamate, are released. The abundance of these synapses means that teenagers are normally full of brain excitement. However, by the end of their teenage years, there is usually a decrease in this hyperexcitement in the brain. This helps to understand why making decisions while hyperexcited are not necessarily wise choices.

Researchers have also discovered that the hyperexcitement is also correlated to a shorter attention span. Impulses and external stimuli are garnering the attentions of our national's children like never before. The rate at which technological stimuli are affecting the brains of students in schools is astounding. Ask any teacher and there will be general agreement.

The emergence of technology is causing brains to speed up and thus bypass the seconds needed for processing accurately. Add this to the state of excitement and emotional heights and the brain remains in a constant state of chemical fluctuation. Thus, teaching in such an environment can be a challenge.

Teenage Contexts

In focusing on teenagers, it becomes quite clear that they contextualize their world through their emotions. For example, the music they listen to places them within contexts. Videos of school events and texts about each other place them in a world that is contextually all about them—and this placement is immediate and comes with emotional reactions, as well as gratification or despair.

Regardless of the contexts—and we all experience them—once a long-term memory is written, the stored music, videos, and texts may provide gateways to reliving the experiences through memory some time in their future. Don Campbell illustrates the impact of music and its use in therapies and healing of brain injuries in his book *The Mozart Effect*.[3] Adult brains use contexts in similar ways. Music naturally brings emotional reactions for most adults and many of these moments were formed in their developing brains as teenagers and children.

Teenagers' first major arguments with friends are emotional contexts and so are their first relationships. An event categorizes a period in time and enables the brain to lay down memories of the event, which helps in the formation of EI.[4] Events are laid down with the assistance of the amygdalae, the twin emotional centers of the brain. It is within these that the contexts of emotions and memories find enrichment in the brain.

The speed at which digital events come to students today cause difficulty in sorting out context, meaning, and even whether there is humor involved. For example, the addition of technology sometimes causes students to be unable to decipher whether an emoticon, or emoji, implies something toward them or an agreement with them.

A brain with many emotionally based learned experiences, coupled with excellent recall of those experiences, is said to be a healthy brain. These are also signs of intelligence.[5] Brains that experience little to no emotion during learning will have less recall. The implications for teachers at this juncture are important. Consider how teachers instruct in middle and high schools and the memories made with students. Memories increase tremendously with the engagement of students' amygdalae. This understanding has formed much of the theories and practices that underlie the push for social-emotional learning (SEL), the newest of comprehensive approaches in public education.

PEAKS OF MATURATION

William Hudspeth and Kurt Fischer have discovered that the teenage brain is still *wiring up* and that there are certain growth surges that mark this wiring. The three general periods of brain-growth surges—or *spurts*—occur between the ages of (1) ten and twelve, (2) fourteen and sixteen, and (3) eighteen and twenty—the latter sometimes extending into the mid-twenties.

Hudspeth and Fischer each performed separate studies yet drew similar conclusions. Hudspeth's study involved 561 Swedish subjects, ages one to twenty-one, and identified "three different peaks of brain maturation during adolescence. These peaks generalize into the following age groups: age twelve, age fifteen, and age eighteen and one-half."[6] Hudspeth discovered a very high correlation between his Swedish students and Jean Piaget's "formal-operations thinking processes."[7]

Brain Differences and Their Meanings

Neuroscientists have "documented an astonishing array of structural, chemical, and functional variations in the brains of males and females."[8] The older and established views of brain theory assumed that humans were ultimately predisposed to their genetic makeups and would follow predetermined genetic paths as their brains developed. An interesting fact validated by studies is that "some sex differences in the brain arise before a baby draws its first breath."[9] The latest research has led to a more modern view on genetic predisposition theory.

Epigenetic theory states that certain processes occur outside of genes and affect the traits of genes when they are expressed but do not affect the basic DNA of a person. In other words, "it is now established that contrasting, persistent, or traumatic environments can and do change the actions of genes."[10] The implications of this research for teachers are highly significant and should inform their instruction and classroom management strategies. But modern neuroscientists no longer seem to accept that any biological differences have much of a significant impact on male and female brains.

The environments to which we expose our students' developing brains can literally change lives but maybe not in ways that are based in predispositions. British neuroscientist Gina Rippon argues that, in terms of determining gender-based brain differences, "technologies have not always lived up to the hype . . . fMRI imaging data have turned out to be far more complex than initially imagined."[11] Her theory implies that because both boys' and girls' brains activate similarly during circumstances which require a demonstration of empathy, there are few gender differences.[12] The only differences, according to Rippon, are in their reporting of the empathy, which girls perform more often.[13]

The sex culture of America has become much more descriptive within fields of social science and humanities, rather than science. When it comes to the progressive views on brain differences, the modern ideas acknowledge physical differences but, because of brain plasticity, diminish any endeavors to discover differences as moot. According to Rippon, "If you put your boy baby in a truck onesie and your girl in a princess onesie, you're already having an impact."[14] Reasoning like this frames valid scientific discoveries as unacceptable, since plasticity is always the default.

The practical *truth test* is to ask all of America's teachers whether they believe there are any differences in brains of boys and girls. Rippon and others would simply shut down anecdotes by saying, the differences exist because of brain plasticity, parental and cultural socialization, and gender stereotypes placed on the boys and girls early on. The challenges for Rippon and others asserting such conclusions come in the following questions: (1) How does any theory adjust to change about gender and sex when it is not allowed to make adjustments to new scientific discoveries? (2) In what ways do theories impact accomplishments in the classrooms each day, given the enormity of the tasks teachers must undertake in terms of instruction and classroom management?

In the sex culture of America, one can see how views like Rippon's lend themselves to gender fluidity and nonbinary identities and promote both cultural and societal imbalance. Confused students do not learn well. Furthermore, what these views must consider—and yet they do not—is the very set of factors that influence children to determine they are one gender or another or prefer even one sexual orientation or another.

On the one hand, neuroscientists and sociologists inform us that boys' and girls' brains are similar. On the other hand, others in the same fields indicate important brain differences, even *in utero*. What is interesting on the ground level regarding the direction of much of this type of discussion is the preponderance of females making interesting determinations about males.

GETTING TO KNOW STUDENTS

How close is too close in getting to know students? Cultural progressives seem very concerned about students' personal sex lives and their gender and sexual understanding of themselves. They demonstrate this concern by asking about oral and vaginal sex and homosexual attraction in surveys.[15] Are these things actually in the best interests for student to reveal to teachers?

Surveys like these, along with discussions in classrooms, are open doors of curiosity for children. It seems that opening these doors—especially with the views on sex, plasticity, and gender that are currently being taught in public schools—that such an impact on children's brains would be just the sort of thing psychologists and sociologists might not support.

Teachers who understand their students have a distinct advantage in the area of relationships. However, the application of this advantage could become problematic. Would teachers develop inappropriate relationships, either emotionally or physically, with students if they knew what the research indicates about long-lasting trauma on the student? Trauma-informed instruction is becoming a staple in teacher education institutions, yet numbers of teachers arrested for inappropriate relationships with students continue to climb.

Some educators believe teacher education institutions must continually remind teacher candidates that they will have very important influences over the literal cognitive and emotional health of their students. Others think most teacher education programs merely mention the issue in passing and move on to focus on student SEL and the practice of restorative justice.

Carrion, Garrett, and Menon write about the effects of trauma on youth, addressing a very sensitive but important issue:

> Children who experience maltreatment and development posttraumatic-stress systems (PTSS) may manifest cognitive and behavioral systems and physiological hyperarousal. These systems may interfere with their ability to process information, especially when related to traumatic events. . . . It has been hypothesized that physiological arousal facilitates self-injurious behaviors (SIB) in children with history of interpersonal trauma. In fact . . . youth with PTSS are significantly more likely to have attempted suicide and have suicidal ideation, and adults with PTSS show an association between impulsivity and suicide risk. . . . History of trauma and posttraumatic symptoms have been associated with self-cutting, the most common form of SIB.[16]

Teachers assume great responsibility. Many students look to teachers to assist them, guide them, and provide a sense of healthy grounding to the real world. The truth is that some teachers come from similar traumatic backgrounds from their youth. Some have overcome their pasts, while others have not. Teachers should understand generally how students' brains function and how each will deal with situations from emotional and cognitive vantage points. Learning more about how students are wired could also assist teachers in coming to understand the effects of certain traumas in their lives.[17]

Navigation of Learning

Males and females navigate learning quite differently. Although not a popular perspective among some social science researchers, many studies suggest that male brains tend to find direction through circumstances by "estimating space and orientation," something referred to in neuroscience as *dead reckoning*. Women, on the other hand, are most likely to navigate their circumstances by monitoring certain landmarks, often through their emotions.[18] Neuroscientists now understand that males and females even process the same emotional memories very differently. This means that the phrase *I love you* uttered by a male after a very romantic date processes into his memory quite differently than it is likely to process into the memory of the female.

At the end of the date, the male might remember the way she looked, her smile, and the emotions and feelings he felt when she touched his hand. The female, though, would probably remember his shoes, the color of his shirt, the table and location where they sat, and the emotional sense derived from noticing an elderly couple at an adjacent table who were celebrating their fiftieth wedding anniversary with smiles and laughter. Males and females process emotions differently and the ways they learn are accomplished differently.

NEUROSCIENCE FOR TEACHERS

One of the reasons for differences in emotional memories between males and females is the result of their biological differences. Although somewhat contrary to political correctness, women possess "significantly larger orbito-frontal amygdalae ratios (OAR) than men do. One can speculate from these findings that women might on average prove [less impulsive and] capable of controlling their emotional reactions."[19]

In females, the amygdalae are the centerpieces of the brain's emotions in humans. Neuroscientists have intensified their study via newer technology, such as positron-emission tomography scans, and the results about brain differences have raised some eyebrows. For example, the hippocampus (working memory) works jointly with the amygdalae (basis of emotions) to assist in learning and transfer to the cerebrum (long-term memory storage).[20] The key for educators of both females and males is to teach so that transfer of knowledge takes place more regularly through instruction that considers the learning differences and brain function.

Male and Female Developmental Characteristics

Developing male brains have more cortical areas dedicated to spatial-mechanical functioning and use about one-half the brain space that females use for verbal-emotive function.[21] This development is one reason why males desire to move objects through space. Most males will experience words and feelings differently than females.[22]

Male brains have less serotonin than female brains. As a result, males are likely to be more physically impulsive and less likely to sit and show empathy to a friend.[23] Furthermore, developing male brains operate with less blood flow than females' brains and tend to compartmentalize learning.[24]

The male brains configure to renew themselves by recharging and reorienting within what neuroscientists call a *rest state*. This is a reason why teenage males tend to drift off during tasks that are not spatial and are often asleep in the back of the class.[25]

Developing female brains have 25 percent more corpus callosum—the bundle of connecting tissue between brain hemispheres—than do males' brains.[26] This enables "cross-talk" between brain hemispheres. It also increases the ability to multitask and the demonstration of better verbal and emotionally based functions.[27]

Female brains have stronger temporal-lobe connectors than male brains. This means that female brains allow for better sensual, detailed memory storage.[28] Furthermore, females tend to multitask better than males, with fewer issues arising from attention-span concerns. This enables females to be less impulsive than males, in general.[29]

The brains of females have larger hippocampus areas than male brains, leading to an advantage in the language arts. The hippocampus is critical in significance, in terms of working memory, in that it assists in the association and retrieval of long-term memories, based on experiences, and emotions.[30] Female and male brains have very significant differences.

Children Are Not Little Adults

As children grow there are unique moments where learning occurs in leaps and bounds. There is a time when the human body is growing so quickly that the stages through which it progresses are awkward and sometimes unexplainable. These are the teenage years and these years comprise a unique period. Raging emotions, verbal confrontations, boredom, and exhilaration can occur at a moment's notice.

Remember those moments when a teenager was asked why he or she acted a certain way or uttered those shocking words? Consider the following hypothetical conversations.

Dad: Why did you do that?

Son: I don't know.

Dad: What were you thinking when you said that?

Daughter: I don't know.

Teacher: What prompted you to do that?

Student: I'm not sure.

Adults generally believe teenagers are calculating and knowledgeable about all of their youthful actions. The natural inclination of the adult is application of adult logic, connecting actions and words to motivation and choice. Most adults understand that there are reasons for what people say and do. Consequently, proclaim adults, there must be a series of connections to thoughts and actions. It would benefit all to remember that children are not little adults, even if their physiology appears adult-like.

There is a certain inescapable logic about *adult thinking*. Adult conclusions are drawn from emotions that have previous contexts. Adult brains are generally calmer and better-wired. Adults draw conclusions based on their deductions from experiences, and these conclusions are sometimes referred to as *gut-level* or *intuitive*. Teenagers lack experience for this to be a reliable part of their decision-making. Thus, they rely more on emotions, feelings, and novel experiences that lack any historical or experiential contexts.

Frontal Lobes

The frontal lobes of human brains are those areas where impulses are generally controlled. Neuroscientists stipulate that the frontal lobes are not fully developed in young people—especially males—until about twenty to twenty-five years of age. That would explain why some teenage females seem to have their impulses under control somewhat earlier than some males.

There is no standardized age for frontal-lobe maturity. Yet we now know there are different degrees of biological development for female and male teenagers. For example, teenage behaviors have direct effects on relationships during the teenage years. Emotional *crushes* are examples of relationships exploded into pleasure by emotions and sometimes imploded into despair by the same. Teenagers crush on people and objects, including teachers. This should draw the attention of every teacher concerned about the nature and depth of their connections with students.

Everything Neuro?

The implications for teachers and teacher education institutions are significant. Brain-based learning is nothing new. Everyone understands that the brain is where learning occurs. Yet what is new is that science and research technology have discovered many physiological aspects as to how the brain learns and that neurogenesis—the making of new brain cells—occurs in us all.[31] Neuroscientist and teacher Judy Willis explains this important discovery:

> For today's students, educators are the lifeline they need to climb for access to the playing fields of twenty-first-century opportunity, open only to those who acquire the necessary skillsets. Teachers who are prepared with knowledge of the workings of the brain will have the optimism, incentive, and motivation to follow the ongoing research and to apply their findings to the classroom.
>
> One example is the research about the brain's neuroplasticity and the opportunities we have as educators to help students literally change their brains—and intelligence. To become a teacher without understanding the implications of brain-changing neuroplasticity is a great loss to teachers and their future students.[32]

An area within the broader discipline of neuroscience is neuroethics. Michael Gazzaniga defines *neuroethics* as "the examination of how we want to deal with the social issues of disease, normality, mortality, lifestyle, and the philosophy of living informed by our understanding of underlying brain mechanisms."[33] Gazzaniga is proclaimed as one of the primary advocates for cognitive neuroscience and the split-brain theory.[34]

Some would argue that this is the basis of much of social action today, primarily when emotions are involved. Digging deeply into students' understanding reveals much about their thoughts, their values, and the extensions of thought processes. There are amazing connections between emotions and learning, and educators are learning more about student motivation and achievement and what emotions trigger each.

Recent research led neuroscientists Jay Giedd[35] and Richard Restak[36] to conclude that "teenagers have the passion and the strength but no brakes." Laurence Steinberg refers to the extremes of teenagers' emotions as "a car with a good accelerator but a weak brake. With powerful impulses under poor control, the likely result is a crash. And, perhaps, a crime."[37]

Sylwester agrees: "The adolescent brain is very sensitive to pleasure and reward, but the impulse-control systems aren't yet mature. Adolescents are thus vulnerable to exploration with highly rewarding drugs—and alcohol/drugs affect the adolescent brain much more than an adult brain."[38] As a result, psychologists today are highly concerned about the "significant overlap between online versus offline relationships and communications among young people. For most adolescents, mobile devices have become a tool for engaging in routine exchanges with friends and strengthening existing relationships. However, mobile technologies have also introduced new tools for bullying."[39]

Brain-Based Instruction

David Sousa writes, "Teachers, of course, hope their students will permanently remember what was taught. Therefore, it is intriguing to realize that the two structures in the brain mainly responsible for long-term remembering are located in the *emotional* area of the brain."[40] Students remember stories and songs so well because their developing brains go way beyond data.

As a result of the work of educators such as Sousa[41] and Eric Jensen,[42] educators have been able to apply brain-based instructional strategies within their classroom. In the past, methods such as Dataworks' Explicit Direct Instruction[43] and the emphasis on common formative assessments[44] resulted in brain research outcomes applicable to student learning and aligned with assessments. More recently, the ideas of student learning styles, fixed, and/or growth mindsets have fallen out-of-style among brain researchers. That is not to say that anyone of these is irrelevant, but researchers claim there is "no benefit to matching a student's perceived learning style—such as visual or linguistic—to the ways a concept can be learned. Instead teachers should focus on tried-and-true strategies such as combining text with pictures, which is superior to presenting either one alone."[45]

Willis introduces the importance of teachers connecting the value of neuroscience and its application to student learning:

> The most valuable assets for improving education won't be developed in a neuroimaging laboratory. It will be educators, with the foundational knowledge about the science of learning, who will be prepared to evaluate the validity and potential educational correlations from neuroscience research. . . . Teachers will be . . . frontline professionals who . . . recognize potential applications of . . . research and develop the strategies that bring the benefits of this research to their students.[46]

Science, education, and new data are making significant impacts on education, in terms of reforming the way teaching and learning take place.

However, those who work with middle- and high-school students know quite well that despite their physical maturity and varying degrees of adult-like behaviors, many students are still emotionally fragile. Hopefully, as teachers, there is the awareness that hyperarousal does not always equate to hyper-maturity and subsequent behavioral balance, and adjustments are made in consideration of these.

Sadly, a reading of the daily headlines reveals all too often that some teachers exploit teenage fragility. These teachers exploit for personal gratification. Evidence of this exploitation occurs at the formation of adult-like romantic and emotional relationships with students. Some students might project that they are ready for such relationships. However, readiness by impulse does not equate to readiness in thoughtful, emotionally mature, and deliberate choices. Teachers must always remind themselves that impulsivity is the driver of teenage decisions. Teachers should beware to tread lightly into the emotional zones of teenage students[47] and reject their own impulses to respond in kind to teenage hyperarousal.

EMOTIONAL INTELLIGENCE

Several common emotions are hardwired into our brains from very early on. As Sylwester points out, "Our six primary emotions are happiness, sadness, surprise, fear, disgust, and anger—and we can add many secondary emotions to that list (such as anticipation, tension, and pride). All [the emotions] are involved in the emotionally important cognitive-arousal systems that must be developed and maintained for our brain to recognize dangers and opportunities. It's a use-it-or-lose-it proposition."[48]

Teachers who connect with students emotionally must take into account various levels of emotional maturity. Teachers who move into inappropriate emotional and physical relationships with students at any level are connecting with students in ways that will probably result in damage to the young person's health, emotional growth, and interpersonal relationships. Besides being morally wrong and illegal, this damage carries over into adulthood and can manifest itself in a host of problems within adult relationships—not the least of which is sexual confusion.

Sometimes It Clicks

What educator has not "enjoyed" those moments when a student finally comprehends something with which he or she had struggled? Cognition and understanding are terrific! Comprehension and long-term memory are keys to true learning. But there are key considerations that are definitely worth noting. One of these keys much more occurs in the brains of students than scripted cognitive experiences.

Take an average teenage male who is not fully capable of exercising self-control intrinsically and who is highly impulsive. Place him in a classroom with a gregarious, young, and attractive female teacher whose smile and personality light up the room. What are the chances the young man is thinking about consequences, in terms of socially acceptable behaviors?

Teachers understand that some of the perceptions formed by students through various emotions are accurate, and some are not. What should then be concluded is that students' brains are in regular states of change. This means that their brains are three to four times more excited at their emotional centers than are adult brains.

As a result of this excitement teenagers are not often basing their cognitive and emotional perceptions on reality. Jensen asserts:

> Adolescence is a wild ride for everybody. . . . There are fast-moving rapid and dramatic changes in biology, cognition, emotion, and interpersonal relationships. . . . Many areas of the brain are under major construction during adolescence. . . . It's safe to call the teen years a "sensitive period." . . . Larger delayed rewards are valued less than smaller immediate rewards. . . . Kids seek higher levels of novelty and stimulation to achieve the same feeling of pleasure. Risks, rewards, and fun are driving their brains.[49]

The fact is that, particularly with middle- and high-school students, they are all over the map in terms of their cognition and emotion. This causes them to be highly susceptible to the words, actions, and expressions of others in the formation of memories. Memories are malleable, and this means emotions are as unique as the memories prompted by them. The adult brain values its memories. People can experience memories over and over again, as brains rely on these memories to make connections to the present. This realization could portend serious ramifications for teachers in their choices of words and actions.

Factors of EI

The physical differences between male and female brains are well documented. Researchers have detected general differences also in EI. Theorist Daniel Goleman illustrates these differences:

> Emotional intelligence has four parts: self-awareness, managing our emotions, empathy, and social skill. There are many tests of emotional intelligence, and most seem to show that women tend to have an edge over men when it comes to these basic skills for a happy and successful life. . . . On the other hand, it's

not that simple. For instance, some measures suggest women are on average better than men are at some forms of empathy, and men do better than women do when it comes to managing distressing emotions. . . . Women tend to be better at emotional empathy than men are; in general . . . neuroscientists tell us one key to empathy is a brain region called the insula. . . . Here's where women differ from men. If the other person is upset, or the emotions are disturbing, women's brains tend to stay with those feelings. But men's brains do something else: they sense the feelings for a moment then tune out of the emotions and switch to other brain areas that try to solve the problem that's creating the disturbance.

Thus, women's complaint that men are tuned out emotionally, and men's that women are too emotional—it's a brain difference. . . . The male tune-out works well when there's a need to insulate yourself against distress. . . . And the female tendency to stay tuned in helps enormously to nurture and support others. . . . It's part of the "tend-and-befriend" response to stress.[50]

EI Varies between Genders

Somewhat recent education trends have focused on *emotional intelligence* and its role in learning. According to Goleman, there are four major factors involved in developing, maintaining, and demonstrating EI. These include (1) intrinsic and extrinsic motivation, (2) impulse control, (3) empathy, and (4) social competence.[51] Each factor assists in the development of mature EI.[52] Most students are somewhere along the pathway of development, which sets them apart from most of their teachers.

Intrinsic and Extrinsic Motivations

Intrinsic motivation "emerges from an environment that encourages students to discover and explore areas of personal interest and ability."[53] It comes from the students' own impulses for experiences. Teachers should ask themselves how to determine what motivates the students on any given day?

First teachers must find ways to produce relevance to what is being taught. Students must see how this teaching fits into their world. Learning that is emotional is fun learning. Fun learning is a motivator in and of itself. The point of emphasis in learning which involves the emotional bases of students' brains is the potential set of affects upon motivation, drive, and passion for additional learning.

Second, teachers have to adjust to being challenged by their students. It is not uncommon in any generation to hear the comments, *why do we have to learn this stuff?* And *when are we ever going to use this in the real world?* Their brains just do not realize or sense the connection. The savvy teacher can answer these two questions with the reply *brain research shows that you need this in order to continue on into cognitive and emotional maturity.*

Grades make things relevant to students. Moreover, teacher feedback is an essential part of student achievement and will always be of high value to their learning curve.[54] Grades contextualize learning. Teachers control the grading and thus become part of the context of whatever emotions arise. But teachers can work beyond emotions with great feedback. From this feedback, a professional relationship can grow, which may yield benefits to students in continued maturation in motivation and confidence.

Impulse Control

In terms of middle- and high-school students, actions can occur without any time devoted to thinking through the risks they are taking. Teenagers, generally, are a bit slower in connecting consequences to behaviors, because the risk is heavily outweighed by the reward of taking the risk.

Risk-taking is part of impulsivity which is a turn-on to many students' brains. Whether in class or with their peers out-and-about, teenagers often do not contemplate their actions ahead of time. The dynamics associated with group thrills usually result from emotions and brain-chemical highs.

Brain Chemicals and Effects on Teenagers

Erin Walsh shares a fairly common occurrence in the following family anecdote.

> I can still remember the kitchen conversation as my brothers excitedly hatched the plan with their friends. "Yes! Let's do it!" was the consensus as five teenage boys raced out the front door with their skateboards. Ten minutes later a neighbor was on the phone asking if my parents knew that there were teenagers, including their two sons, skate boarding down twenty Fourth Street tethered by rope to a car.
>
> Later, as my parents grilled my brothers with, "What were you thinking?!" my brothers looked fairly disinterested in the lecture. Reminding them of the potential for broken bones or worse brought the familiar rolling of the eyes.[55]

In many ways, this is an example of classic teenage behavior, illustrating the kind of risk-taking and thrill-seeking long associated with adolescence. For a long time a scene like this would have been chalked up to raging hormones and inexplicably immature logic. More recently, however, science has helped us better understand the neurological basis of risky adolescent behavior.

Brain chemicals have much to do with the ways teenagers form bonds with others, as well as the ways they act. Teenagers are biochemically impassioned. There are five basic brain chemicals and these influence on teenage students' behaviors. The five chemicals in questions are (1) noradrenaline (or epinephrine),[56] (2) dopamine,[57] (3) serotonin,[58] (4) glucose,[59] and (5) cortisol.[60]

The abundance or shortage of these chemicals can indicate maturity or immaturity. The impact of either of these conditions has ramifications upon classroom-learning environments. Behavior impulses normally associate with the broader discussion of maturity. Neuroscientists, such as Jay Giedd, conclude that teens are normally full speed ahead in many of their choices, crushes, and connections,[61] based on one or more of the chemicals released in the brain. The following paragraphs provide a brief description and application of the five basic brain chemicals.

Noradrenaline (Norepinephrine)

Students called on in class, or faced with a series of choices in front of their peers, are awash with chemicals. They must choose to either participate or not participate. Either choice involves some degree of stress. If students enjoy working on projects in small groups, one can expect brain chemicals, usually referred to as *adrenalines* (including dopamine), to be at high levels.

Teachers who structure their classrooms so that there are never any risks to be taken, or that no pressures are experienced, will find students describing the class and teacher as *boring, unchallenging*, and *impractical*. Teaching strategies that press limits of healthy risk-taking provide a host of benefits for students. Assisting students in risk-taking provides excellent groundwork for what most students can expect to experience in their adult lives.

Dopamine

Students who find pleasure in life's experiences and in their relationships with people have good levels of dopamine. Students who seek one emotionally high experience after another are experiencing regular rushes of dopamine. If asked to settle down in a classroom, these students will find it difficult to learn without certain levels of excitement built in. The high energy teacher, whose classroom includes higher rigors and displays a deep passion for her students and for learning, will begin to see students finding pleasure in the same.

When something is *fun* to a student, dopamine helps the brain to relate it as enjoyable. Conversely, when there are negative experiences involved, dopamine is also at work, seeking to regulate the pain involved. The classroom environment plays a crucial role in the regulation of dopamine levels in teenagers. The average person usually refers to dopamine as the *adrenaline rush*.

Serotonin

Serotonin helps to regulate moods, desire for sleep, and even digestion. Getting students up and about the classroom assists in the creation of serotonin.

In other words, too little serotonin, the student is drowsy. Physical movement in the classroom and interaction with others is healthy.

Small-group conversations, accompanied by students' physical movements, help in the reduction of states associated with negative emotions and anxiety for teenagers. Getting students up and about during learning is equally as healthy for younger children as it is for teenagers. It is also one reason why adults with jobs that either require physical movement or require working for employers that promote employee wellness tend to be in better moods.[62]

Glucose

Glucose (blood sugar) and fat work together with cortisol to produce energy in our bodies. Teenagers whose glucose levels drop—because of skipping a meal or lack of physical exercise—are going to be hampered by an eventual lack of energy and motivation. Physical movement and exertion help to create glucose. Again, whatever teachers can do to incorporate student movement about the classroom, at pivotal times during the class period, will help with energy levels and production of glucose and other chemicals vital for maximizing their classroom time.

Cortisol

Cortisol works together with glucose to provide energy for students. Glucose also uses stored fat to help the body manage stress. This stress is from pressures put on students not just by teachers but by life in general. The stress is also physical. Therefore, athletes and academic competitors are candidates for increased production of cortisol, working in tandem with glucose. Teaching students how to manage stress means to instruct them on balancing their lives and getting plenty of exercise and rest, so that their brains and bodies are balanced, avoiding an abundance of any one chemical for prolonged periods. This is precisely why teachers should recommend their students not be online late into the evening hours or spend excessive time using smart technology by pulling all-nighters playing the latest popular video game. Such behaviors cause exhaustion as the brain continues the flow of chemicals at hours when the body and brain need rest.

Empathy

Empathy is an important emotional expression for children to learn. It derives from EI, which coincides with the brain's developing frontal lobes. Empathy allows students to act in ethical ways and demonstrate altruism, which is why many teenagers care so much about their friends and others, the nature and animals around them, and the environment. Fairness is a serious issue for empathetic teenagers, made all the more obvious when they stand up for their friends in class.

Teachers can help teenagers and their peers in the development of empathy by allowing students to share their thoughts and allow their experiences with empathy to connect with those of others. Sometimes writing is a way for students to express their thoughts. Teachers ought to be aware of the tool they possess in student empathy but avoid using empathy to manipulate students' emotions for an agenda or selfish reasons or to step over the line of propriety. The following are two contrasting examples.

First, imagine a teacher with a strong political or social agenda, purposefully playing to the emotions of students. The chances are great that the teacher will win many to the issue being advocated. Teachers manipulate students in thousand ways that are healthy and appropriate. Telling the truth and earning students' trust in the most unbiased way possible is a great learning tool in the teaching of empathy. The following personal anecdote is derived from my youth and illustrates an expression of empathy.

As a fifteen-year-old, my mode of transportation was a homemade bicycle. Mismatched tires, fabricated handlebars, and a banana seat made up my pride and joy. My friends and I were always making things together, and our bicycles were among our crowning achievements. We rode everywhere on our bicycles, often taking lengthy day trips for fun.

One day, my friends and I went on a long bike ride to see my grandmother. She lived in Towaco, New Jersey, sixteen miles away one way, which meant navigating some very busy roads. Somewhere about halfway into our trip, which began in Bloomfield, New Jersey, we braked to a stop at a four-way highway intersection. As we impatiently straddled our bikes, waiting for the light to change in our favor, a couple of us noticed a small kitten standing in the intersection. We also noticed that it was in the direct path of a turning semi-tractor trailer. Within seconds, all of my friends noticed the kitten and began to yell at the driver to stop. However, it was too late. One of the rear wheels of the truck clipped the kitten's body. "Oh, no!" many of us yelled.

I quickly dropped my bike and ran out into the traffic. One of my friends raised his hands for cars to stop. I scooped up the writhing kitten and cupped her in my palms and then ran to my friends. One of them said, "Put her down; she's almost dead anyway." However, I couldn't put her down. Her bright green eyes were teary. She struggled to breathe. She mustered enough strength to release a couple of high-pitched mews. Within seconds, the tiny kitten shuddered in my hands, went limp, and died. I had never seen anything or anyone die, or even dead before, and I was at a loss as to what to do. So I laid her partially mangled body against the curb at the intersection and rode off with tears in my eyes.

Social Competence

Social competence is that which allows students to *read* social contexts and then respond appropriately. Teenagers are often socially awkward, particularly when singled out, or in the beginning stages of relationships with persons they care deeply about. They seek to fit in, while removing the need to justify the fit. Teenagers find identity by dressing like each other. Haircuts, taste in music, youthful language, and teenage activities and games are all points of identity for students and demonstrate levels of social competency.

Teenagers are attuned to social competence in relation to each other in greater fashion than they are in terms of relationships with adults. This truism bears direct relevance to the topic of this book. Socially mature adults and awkward social students are not meant to be in emotional or physical relationships. There is no socially competent meeting of the minds or emotions.

USING EMOTIONS TO CREATE MEMORIES

Recall the father who made national headlines and became a YouTube viral sensation. His fifteen-minute on-camera reading and recording drew all sorts of attention. Essentially, what the father did was read his fifteen-year-old teenage daughter's profanity-filled Facebook posts, one at a time. He told her not to post personal feelings about the family, yet she persisted. As a result, the father took extreme measures.

As the father sat outside on a lawn chair, calmly reading his daughter's posts on camera, he would pause briefly, at times, to provide his own profanity-laced comments. When finished, he took out a pistol and shot several bullets into his daughter's laptop computer, which lay on the ground next to his chair. All of this was broadcast for the world to view. The video went viral, which means millions upon millions of viewers watched it.

Shooting and *killing* a computer, as a point to be made, is something the teenager will never forget. The incident was memorable and certainly touched the emotions. However, what was learned in the process? This is no way to relate to a teenager the message that her disobedience in posting profanity and angry language against her family was unacceptable. The father's actions were just as unacceptable as what the daughter had done. These are extremes and are never the best methods for modeling appropriate behaviors. However, the father's goal of imprinting an extreme emotional memory was realized.

Here is another example of creating a memory through extremism. This time the event occurred in the classroom. Some years ago, a junior-high colleague was teaching a unit on terrorism. A colleague had a friend dress up in black clothing and a mask and come into his classroom to hold his students hostage. There was no weapon involved, only the imaginations of teenagers and words of a terrorist impostor. The surprise element resulted in shrieks, and some of the students screamed out of shock and fear.

This incident was also memorable because it was extreme by playing on the fears of students. If memorable is the ultimate goal by any means, then learning is compromised by emphasizing trauma. Likewise, if emotional reactions are the focal point, then one experience is merely replaced by another more extreme experience.

These types of tactics are as inappropriate as they are memorable. That was the conclusion drawn by the principal and many of the parents. Teachers should try to remember the *son or daughter rule*. Would it be appropriate for another teacher to do or say to my own child what I plan to do or say to this student? We must remember that students will remember strong emotional experiences.

Building Memories as Social Creatures

Humans are social creatures. Our brains connect in ways that allow language, expression, feelings, and various other methods of relationship building to take place.[63] Sylwester concurs: "We're a social species, and so much of our cognitive strength comes from our ability to successfully understand and interact with others. Frontal-lobe areas . . . play key roles in developing and regulating social behavior."[64] Social connections, resulting in social behaviors, are part of the norm for social creatures. Social activists understand this well.

Immordino-Yang and Damasio maintain that humans are "fundamentally emotional and social creatures." However, they add implications to these fundamentals, concluding that

> some in the field of education often fail to consider that the high-level cognitive skills taught in schools, including reasoning, decision making, and processes related to language, reading, and mathematics, do not function as rational, dis-embodied systems, somehow influenced by but detached from emotion and the body. . . . Any competent teacher recognizes that emotions and feelings affect students' performance and learning, as does the state of the body. . . . We contend . . . that the relationship between learning, emotion, and body state runs deeper that many educators realize and is interwoven with the notion of learning.[65]

LOVE AND EMOTIONAL MATURITY

What does the average student know about love? If you ask any of them this question, they will respond with *I know a lot*. The response *I know a lot* indicates they have some knowledge about love, but little actual understanding.

For example, the average middle or high schooler, when asked *to explain the differences between unconditional love and conditional love,* is going to draw a blank. What teenagers proclaim to know and what they profess to understand are two different realities. They sometimes confuse knowledge with understanding. They are not alone. In fact, some adults are still trying to figure this out, as well. This is another reason why this book is such a necessity for today's teachers.

Teenagers view videos and how-to presentations and observe sex and romance in the media, and sometimes they believe the ideals and feelings demonstrated across culture, and on screen, comprise the depths of love. Many Hollywood movie endings leave us feeling good. Why is all of this a concern for teachers and their relationships with students?

Emotions can easily make people appear foolish. Teenagers' emotions fool them into believing there is depth of emotional maturity merely because they feel more deeply and are aware of emotions like never before. This gets back to novelty experiences, where newness may be equated to near epiphanies, and when emotions are the defining moments of truth, there may be trouble ahead.

Even empathy can fool teenagers into a sense of caring that may be a bit overblown. It has already been established that what teenagers perceive as their feelings may not be based in reality. Students should be on guard not to conclude that their feelings on matters of personhood are not final arbiter of their true identities. Likewise, teachers should exercise caution not to hold students to these feelings, as some form of absolute, especially in an age of rapidly shifting moral compasses.

Modern culture bombards all of us with sexual images, often aimed directly at teenagers. However, not all sexual pressures aim at youth. Mostly everyone wants to be sexually attractive and alluring these days. There are matchmaking sites for adults from ages eighteen to ninety-eight. We are told to be sexy at any age. Clothing and music converge upon the sensual and gravitate toward the sexual. Advertisers are using sexual imagery in ways that include young children.

Pornography seems to be everywhere online and easily accessible. Parents should engage in regular discourse with their children about sexuality. If they do not, they might not like the sources that step in to provide their own sex culture versions of sexuality. That said, parents should not be surprised if teenagers pick up their knowledge from sources that seek more from them than their visual and auditory attention. Unfortunately, students are learning more about sex from teachers these days.

Some argue that teenagers are more mature today because of exposure to adult-like materials. This is not true. Advocates of that position are either naïve or have not worked with teenagers long enough to analyze their actions to understand their brain development and the characteristics that comprise a lack of emotional maturity. Exposure does not equate to maturity.

Teenagers cannot be any more mature than their brains and bodies allow them to be. They exist in awkward physical and emotional states. Teachers must never assume that the external visages of students or their emotional connections with students are somehow equivalent to a revelation so unique that it extends beyond the chronological ages of the students.

Students' bodies and brains are not yet in alignment, chronologically and biologically, for adult maturity to occur. Perception is not reality, except that it is a real perception. The bottom line is teachers who mistake well-developed teenagers as having arrived at maturity must stop to consider that the outside does not match the inside.

When it comes to love, do teenagers have the capacity to really understand this word as an adult would expect? Are students aware that there are many expressions of love? Compared to the images of "love" crammed into their ocular portals, is there any deeper understanding beyond the physical or feelings of sexual excitement?

There are many types of love and even more expressions of love than a person can count—and only one of these types focuses exclusively on sex. This is the love that bombards Americans daily. The rising tide of sexuality threatens to drown out virtues such as empathy, patience, and kindness, and detracts from concepts such as unconditional commitment—all of which have their basis in types of love. This is why all Americans must question why their children's teacher could ever expect to grow an adult-like relationship with a sixteen- or seventeen-year-old.

In every generation, young people learn to be adults through avenues of experience. But experience is not enough. Having sex with a teacher does not make one an adult. However, it does make one a victim.

How and what students learn depends a lot on the adults in their lives. As Americans navigate through this culture of sex, coupled with smart technology, it is incumbent on adults and people in positions of authority to draw clear moral and ethical lines, and this includes establishing boundaries when it comes to expressions of love.

Teenagers and Expressions of Love

Teenagers' music is flooded with songs about love, often defined as casual sex. Videos demonstrating affections and playing up one's sexuality, as well as their emotions and crushes, are enticing. However, what exactly is the extent of teenagers' understanding about love? The Greek language helps us to understand the different concepts and expressions of love. Deeper conceptual meanings are not always lost when translating ancient words into English.[66]

First, there is *agape* love—a love characterized by unconditional dedication and lifelong expression and not relegated merely to circumstances. It is love that is present in commitment. Teenagers idealize the forever love, even with their innate impulsivity.

A second type of love is found in the concept of *phileo*, a type of brotherly love—whence the city of Philadelphia derived its name (*phileo* = love; *adelphos* = brother). This is the kind of love that rises in support of a sibling wronged by another. This expression comes across as vicarious love, the very expression that accompanies unity in standing with another against a bully or speaking on behalf of a person experiencing an unfair situation.[67]

A third type of love is characterized by the word *storge*. This is the warm, fuzzy type of love. *Storge* is likely the result of a crush, or the love of a family pet, the giving of hugs, and things such as these. One word comes to mind when *storge* is present. That word is *affection*.[68]

This leaves the last type of love as the physical love, *eros*, whence we derive the word *erotic*. This type of love excites the mind and body and prepares it for sexual pleasure. This is where the brain's hyperarousal in teenagers sometimes meets with difficulty. Deciphering between strong physical attraction and expressions of love that accompany the emotions and feelings is often misread. Of these four loves, eros is the one that modern culture elevates in alignment with teenage impulsivity.[69] In addition, it seems to motivate many of the inappropriate physical and sexual relationships teachers are having with their students.

Today's culture focuses almost exclusively on erotic forms of love—the kind of love that does not lead to lifelong commitment in most cases. Eros is not necessarily compatible with meetings of minds or shared emotions or intellects. Eros sparks lusts and passions, growing ever so quickly from emotions to fiery sexual pleasures and mostly aligned with hyperaroused student brains.

Relationships between people who focus their understanding and practice of love on different levels can only lead to frustration. Involving children in this frustration results in the addition of trauma to their lives and detracts from their well-being. Yet is this not precisely where teenagers are subject to deception and manipulation, as adults blur the lines of relational appropriateness?[70]

APPROPRIATE TEACHER-STUDENT RELATIONSHIPS

Relationships play a large part in determining how students fit within the larger context of education. As a result, in terms of teachers and students, three basic tiers address appropriate relationships. These appropriate relationships can be formed individually or in plurality. The three tiers are (1) intraschool academic relationships, (2) intraschool extracurricular relationships, and (3) interpersonal nonschool-related relationships. Figure 1.1 illustrates

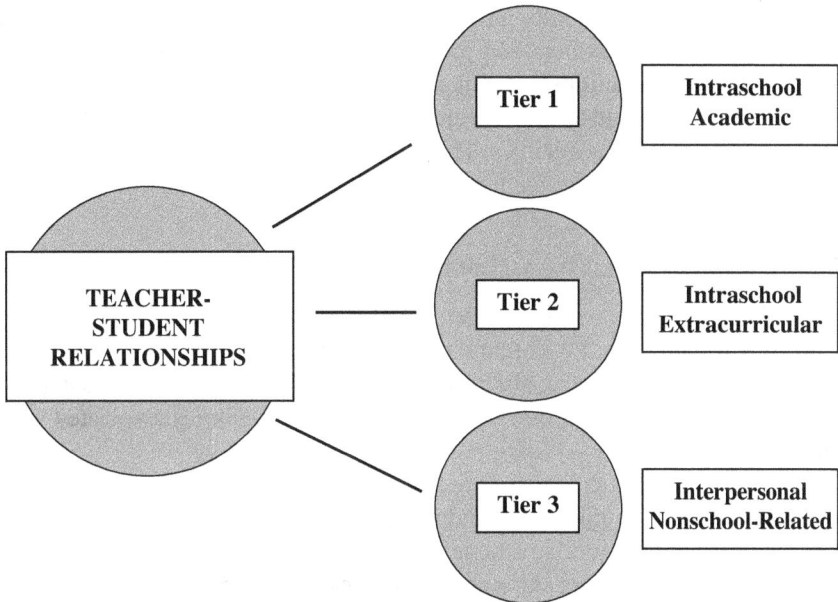

Figure 1.1. Three Tiers of Teacher-Student Relationships
Source: Self-Designed, MS Word

the three different relational tiers that are often enjoyed between teachers and their students.

Tier 1: Intraschool Academic Relationships

Tier 1 intraschool academic relationships are the first-tier relationships and are defined as teacher-student relationships that are tied to the academic institution, whether in classes, through counseling, or in fine arts or any other academic areas related to school. Tier1 relationships are basic relationships that occur in the classroom or within normal school-hour functions, at any grade level and are in alignment with the professional mission of the school. Intrapersonal relationships are significantly different from *inter*personal relationships (which materialize in tier 3), and yet they work together.

Tier 2: Intraschool Extracurricular Relationships

Tier 2 intraschool extracurricular relationships are developed through extracurricular involvement. Coaching, athletics, science fairs, spelling bees, working with academic competitive teams, and organizing and overseeing students at tournaments fall under this heading. These relationships are often extensions of the classroom and involve fewer students and smaller groups. However, tier 2 relationships bring with them the addition of mentoring, character-building and teamwork, and physical or honed skills not necessarily tied to the classroom academics. These relationships can also involve parents and families and are significant to developing annual school pride events.

Tier 3: Interpersonal Nonschool-Related Relationships

Tier3 interpersonal nonschool-related relationships are different from relationships in tiers 1 and 2 in that they are more highly personal, occur away from the school day, and do not usually involve school academics or competitions. Therefore, there are fewer professional responsibilities associated with tier 3 relationships.

Ideally, the three tiers work together as seamlessly as they can, providing a healthy blend of intrapersonal and interpersonal experiences. Depending on the circumstances that arise among teachers, coaches, students, participants, and players, tier 3 relationships can sometimes be very powerful and serve to reinforce other relationships.

BEYOND THE CLASSROOM AND ALWAYS ON DUTY

School culture naturally spills over into the surrounding community. Relationships that develop at school are different than those that develop outside of school, but they are all relationships, nonetheless.[71] Teachers in American high schools who think that after the final school bell rings they are no longer teachers need to read this next section very closely. Union members, take note, as well.

Teachers are never really off duty, even after their contractual hours are fulfilled. If relationships are as vital to the soul of education as many believe they are, this premise is certainly sensible. "Teachers must go beyond the scripts they are handed to learn about what student are and what they care about."[72] It is unpopular to maintain the position that teachers are still on duty after meeting their contractual obligations. Merely suggesting to teachers that they are accountable to local communities and for upholding the reputations of schools is met with strange looks and emotional responses of varying degrees.

In many ways, every person associated with the school is an extension of the school. In this sense, teachers are *still on duty*, as it were, to parents and students wherever they are seen in the community. Teachers are, as Herman and Marlowe refer to as, *servant leaders*, who make caring about students and what can be expected from them their primary concern.[73] Even after graduation from high school, former students refer to teachers—even those long retired—as *my old high school English teacher* or *my former high school soccer coach.*

Something which most teachers probably know but is worth restating is that the largest predictor as to whether students will graduate from high school is whether they have formed any meaningful relationships with their teachers, parents, and friends.[74] Educators must always be mindful that these relationships are appropriate at every turn, for their success or failure impacts lives well into the future.

Parents are still parents, and students are still students—whether they've left school or still sit in classrooms. Any teacher who works with high-school seniors or befriends students or former students on social networking sites knows this feeling well. Titles live on well after hours, into the retirement years and beyond—and so does reputation.

In closing, permit the author the opportunity to reminisce. A teacher friend and I were out for a Saturday run. We had finished exercising and were walking through the parking lot in front of our favorite coffee shop, when across the way we heard, "Hey, Dr. Zarra!" It was one of my students. His father was with him and looked at his son, asking, "Who's that?" Reality truly hit home when he replied, "That's my teacher." From that point on it became clear that once a teacher, always a teacher.

From the students' perspectives, their reality is that teachers are always on duty. And the media also seem to think this is true. Think about any time a teacher is arrested: whether they are at school, on vacation, or out in the community, the person arrested is boldly labeled "teacher" within the headlines.

SUMMARY

Students' brains have an abundance of synapses or regions where transmission and reception of impulses occurs. The abundance of these synapses signifies that teenagers are full of brain excitement. Specifically, teenagers contextualize their world through their emotions. Sometimes these contexts are environmental and their surroundings settle into their memories. Memories increase tremendously with the engagement of students' amygdalae, the emotional centers of the brain.

The latest research in neuroscience is yielding some astounding data. Studies are showing that some gender differences in the brain arise before a baby is even born. Males and females navigate learning quite differently. Additional studies suggest that male brains tend to find direction through circumstances by *estimating space and orientation*, something that neuroscientists refer to as *dead reckoning*. Neuroscientists now understand that males and females process emotional memories very differently.

Adults generally believe teenagers calculate their youthful actions. Adults draw conclusions based on their experiences, and these conclusions are referred to as *gut-level* or *intuitive* conclusions. Those who work with high-school students know quite well that despite their physical maturity and varying degrees of adult-like behaviors, many of them are still emotionally fragile.

Hyperarousal of brains and emotions does not always equate to hypermaturity and effective activity in terms of learning and achievement. Emotions are as unique as the memories prompted by them. For example, the adult brain values its memories. The same emotion is never experienced identically, but our memories make the effort.

Recent education trends have focused on *emotional intelligence* and its role in student learning. Goleman sees four major factors involved in developing, maintaining, and evidencing EI: (1) intrinsic and extrinsic motivation, (2) impulse control, (3) empathy, and (4) social competence.

Brain chemicals have much to do with the way teenagers form bonds with others. The abundance or shortage of these chemicals is indicative of what adults consider maturity. The five brain chemicals discussed in the chapter are (1) noradrenaline (or epinephrine), (2) dopamine, (3) serotonin, (4) glucose, and (5) cortisol. Each has a specific role in learning for both teenagers and adults.

Humans are social creatures. Our brains connect in ways that allow language, expression, feelings, and various other methods of relationship-building. Emotions can fool us, and emotions can rule us! Teenagers' emotions fool them into believing there is depth of emotional maturity merely because they feel more deeply and are aware of emotions like never before. Teenagers cannot be any more mature than their brains and bodies allow them to be. What we call *emotions* are actually complex body/mind states made up of four different sets of physiological and psychological processes.

America's sex culture celebrates erotic forms of love—the kind that does not lead to lifelong commitment in most cases. Physical maturity has its own time clock and so does emotional maturity. Culture often reduces love to feelings and pleasures. Since teenagers do not generally possess the requisite EI and maturity to understand the depths of love, they can easily confuse one form of love with another. Teachers must always keep this in the backs of their minds.

DISCUSSION QUESTIONS

1. How would you define *student maturity*? Provide three examples of behaviors to illustrate the definition.

2. Can you briefly explain how hardwired emotions play into what teenagers and adults remember?
3. What causes teenagers to be impulsive in their actions? What is taking place in their brains to prompt such impulsiveness?
4. Why have neuroscientists concluded that memories are malleable?
5. Given that male and female brains have biological differences in structure and function, how should these differences affect classroom instruction?
6. What is your opinion about Goleman's research on *emotional intelligence*?
7. What are the roles of the chemicals in the teenage brain, and how does each affect behaviors?
8. In what ways are emotions unreliable as the foundation of knowledge and truth in the lives of your students?
9. How has modern technology benefited human social interactions and enhanced human relationships?
10. How would you describe the average student's understanding of the *four loves* addressed in this chapter?

NOTES

1. Eric Jensen. "Emotions in students." *Jensen Learning.* 2013. Retrieved from https://www.jensenlearning.com/emotions-in-students/.

2. Alison Gopnik. "What's wrong with the teenage mind?" *Wall Street Journal.* January 28, 2012. Retrieved from http://online.wsj.com/article/SB100014240529702 03806504577181351486558984.html.

3. Don Campbell. *The Mozart effect.* 1997. New York: Avon Books.

4. Daniel Goleman. *Emotional intelligence.* 1995. New York: Bantam Books.

5. Howard Gardner. *Frames of mind: Theories of multiple intelligences.* 2011. New York: Basic Books.

6. Anita Woolfolk. *Educational psychology,* 10th ed. 2007. San Francisco, CA: Allyn & Bacon, pp. 26–36. Cf. B. Wadsworth. *Piaget's theory of cognitive and affective development,* 5th ed. 1996. Boston, MA: Allyn & Bacon. Retrieved from www. learningandteaching.info/learning/piaget.html.

7. Ibid.

8. Larry Cahill. "His brain, her brain." May 2005. *Scientific American,* p. 41. Cf. Larry Cahill Melina Uncapher, Lisa Kilpatrick, Mike Alkire, and Jessica Turner "Sex-related hemispheric lateralization of amygdala function in emotionally influenced memory: An fMRI investigation." 2004. *Learning and Memory,* p. 3. Cf. also Robert Coles, *The moral intelligence of children.* 1997. New York: Random House Publishers, and M. K. Demaray and C. K. Malecki. "The relationship between perceived social support and maladjustment for students at risk." 2002. *Psychology in the Schools* 39: 305–16.

9. Cahill, "His brain, her brain," p. 42.

10. Eric Jensen, *Enriching the brain*. 2006. San Francisco, CA: Jossey-Bass Publishers, p. 10.

11. Nicole Natri. "Gender and our brains: How new neuroscience explodes the myths of the male and female minds." *The New York Times*. September 9, 2019. Retrieved from https://www.nytimes.com/2019/09/09/books/review/gender-and-our-brains-gina-rippon.html.

12. Ibid.

13. Ibid.

14. Ibid.

15. Staff. "Middle school asks kids personal questions about vaginal sex, oral sex, and homosexual attraction." *Activist Mommy*. September 28, 2019. Retrieved from https://activistmommy.com/middle-school-asks-kids-about-vegetables-bike-helmets-and-oral-and-vaginal-sex/?fbclid=IwAR32LEYlbnErKzC3jd7cJsGF4 7sA-oGq-Zrfrl5xTTSB9CiWX4SiyHCI6UI.

16. Victor G. Carrion et al. "Posttraumatic stress symptoms and brain function during a response-inhibition task: An fMRI study in youth." 2008. *Depression and Anxiety* 25: 514–26. Retrieved from http://med.stanford.edu/nbc/articles/11Posttraumatic%20 stress%20symptoms%20and%20brain%20function%20during%20a%20response-inhibition%20task.pdf.

17. Melanie Greenberg. "How PTSD and trauma affect your brain functioning." *Psychology Today*. September 29, 2018. Retrieved from https://www. psychologytoday.com/us/blog/the-mindful-self-express/201809/how-ptsd-and-trauma-affect-your-brain-functioning.

18. Cahill, "His brain, her brain," p. 44.

19. Ibid. Cf. Deborah Blum, *Sex on the brain: The biological differences between men and women*. 1997. New York: Viking Press.

20. David A. Sousa, *How the brain learns*, 3rd ed. 2006. Thousand Oaks, CA: Corwin Press, pp. 15–24. Cf. Michael Gurian and Kathy Stevens, "With boys and girls in mind." November 2004. *Educational Leadership* 62(3): 21–26. Cf. also Michael Gurian, Patricia Henley, and Terry Trueman. 2001. *Boys and girls learn differently! A guide for teachers and parents*. San Francisco, CA: Jossey-Bass/Wiley Publishers; Michael Gurian. 1996. *The wonder of boys: What parents, mentors, and educators can do to shape boys into exceptional men*. New York: Penguin Books; and Michael Gurian. 2002. *The wonder of girls: Understanding the hidden nature of our daughters*. New York: Atria Books.

21. Sousa, *How the brain learns*.

22. Blum, *Sex on the brain*.

23. Shelley Taylor. *The tending instinct*. 2002. New York: Times Books.

24. Sousa, *How the brain learns*.

25. Gurian et al., *Boys and girls learn differently!*

26. Eric Jensen. 2005. *Teaching with the brain in mind*. Alexandria, VA: Association for Supervision and Curriculum Development.

27. Jay Giedd in Richard Restak. 2001. *The secret life of the brain*. Washington, D.C.: Joseph Henry Press.

28. Jensen *Enriching the brain*, pp. 24 and 31.

29. Giedd in Restak, *The secret life of the brain*.

30. Sousa, *How the brain learns*. See also Jensen, *Enriching the brain*.

31. S. McGillivray and A. Castel, "Betting on memory leads to metacognitive improvement by younger and older adults." 2011. *Psychology and Aging* 26(1): 137–44.

32. Judy Willis. 2009. *How your child learns best: brain-friendly strategies you can use to ignite your child's learning and increase school success*. Napersville, IL: Sourcebooks, Inc. Cf. Judy Willis. 2007. *Brain-friendly strategies for the inclusion classroom*. Alexandria, VA: Association for Supervision and Curriculum Development; cf. also M. Eisenhart and R. L. DeHaan. "Doctoral preparation of scientifically based educational researchers." 2005. *Educational Researcher* 34(4): 3–13 and Judy Willis. "A neurologist makes the case for teaching teachers about the brain." *Edutopia*. July 27, 2012. Retrieved from www.edutopia.org/blog/neuroscience-higher-ed-judy-willis.

33. Michael S. Gazzaniga. 2005. *The ethical brain*. New York: HarperCollins Publishers.

34. Michael S. Gazzaniga. *Tales from both sides of the brain: A life in neuroscience*. 2015. New York: Harper-Collins Publishers.

35. Gopnik, "What's wrong with the teenage mind?"

36. Malcolm Ritter. "Experts link teen brains' immaturity, juvenile crime." *USA Today*. December 2, 2007. Retrieved from www.usatoday.com/tech/science/2007-12-02-teenbrains_N.htm.

37. Laurence Steinberg in Ritter, "Experts link teen brains' immaturity." Cf. Laurence Steinberg. "Adolescent development and juvenile justice." November 28, 2011. Retrieved from http://eji.org/eji/files/Science%20on%20Adolescent%20Development_0.pdf.

38. Robert Sylwester. 2007. *The adolescent brain: reaching for autonomy*. San Francisco, CA: Corwin Press.

39. Madeline J. George and Candice L. Odgers. "The risks and rewards of being an adolescent in the digital age." *American Psychological Society*. December 2014. Retrieved from https://www.apa.org/pi/families/resources/newsletter/2014/12/digital-age.

40. Sousa, *How the brain learns*, p. 19.

41. Ibid.

42. Jensen, *Enriching the brain*.

43. John Hollingsworth and Silvia Ybarra. 2006. *Explicit direct instruction*. Thousand Oaks, CA: Corwin Press. Cf. *Dataworks*. Retrieved from www.dataworks-ed.com/research.

44. Larry Ainsworth and Donald Viegut. 2006. *Common formative assessment: How to connect standards-based instruction and assessment*. Thousand Oaks, CA: Corwin Press. Cf. Richard DuFour and Robert Eaker. 1998. *Professional learning communities at work*. Bloomington, IN: Solution Tree.

45. Youki Terada. "2018 education research highlights." *Edutopia*. December 7, 2018. Retrieved from https://www.edutopia.org/article/2018-education-

research-highlights. Cf. Eric Jensen. "Jensen learning workshop. 7 discoveries from brain research that impact education." *Jensen Learning*. 2019. Retrieved from https://www.jensenlearning.com/products/7-discoveries-from-brain-research-that-impact-education/.

46. Willis, "*A neurologist makes the case for teaching teachers about the brain.*"

47. Gazzaniga, *The ethical brain.*

48. Robert Sylwester, "Present at the maturation of the adult brain." Paper presented at Learning and the Brain Conference, Stanford University. February 8, 2008, pp. 1–8.

49. Jensen, *Enriching the brain*, pp. 101–2.

50. Daniel Goleman. "Are women more emotionally intelligent than men?" May 6, 2011. Retrieved from http://danielgoleman.info/2011/are-women-more-emotionally-intelligent-than-men/.

51. Daniel Goleman. 1995. *Emotional intelligence: Why it can matter more than IQ*. New York: Bantam Books.

52. Gardner, *Frames of mind.*

53. Sylwester, *The adolescent brain.*

54. Jensen, *Enriching the brain.*

55. Erin Walsh. "The teenage brain: How dopamine spurs risk taking." *Mind Positive Parenting*. November 1, 2016. Retrieved from https://www.youthfrontiers.org/blog-teenage-risk-taking/.

56. "Noradrenaline (Norepinephrine): How does it work?" July 16, 2012. *Retrieved from* www.netdoctor.co.uk/heart-and-blood/medicines/noradrenaline.html.

57. "Dopamine: A sample neurotransmitter." *University of Texas Addiction Science Research Center*. July 16, 2012. Retrieved from www.utexas.edu/research/asrec/dopamine.html.

58. "What is serotonin? What does serotonin do?" *Medical News Today*. August 4, 2011. Retrieved from www.medicalnewstoday.com/articles/232248.php.

59. Roni Caryn Rabin. "Blood sugar control linked to memory decline, study says." *New York Times*. December 31, 2008. Retrieved from www.nytimes.com/2009/01/01/health/31memory.html. Cf. Jane B. Gore, Desiree L. Krebs, and Marise B. Parent. "Changes in blood glucose and salivary cortisol are not necessary for arousal to enhance memory in young or older adults." 2006. *Psychoneuroendocrinology*. 31(5): 589–600. Retrieved from http://pubget.com/paper/16530333/Changes_in_blood_glucose_and_salivary_cortisol_are_not_necessary_for_arousal_to_enhance_memory_in_young_or_older_adults.

60. "Cortisol in blood." W*eb MD*. Retrieved from www.webmd.com/a-to-z-guides/cortisol-14668.

61. Giedd in Restak, *The secret life of the brain.*

62. Alan Kohll. "Why we pay our employees to exercise at work." *Forbes*. January 9, 2019. Retrieved from https://www.forbes.com/sites/alankohll/2019/01/09/why-we-pay-our-employees-to-exercise-at-work/#559243b028d2.

63. G. Rizzolatti. "Mirrors in the mind." October 16, 2006. *Scientific American*, pp. 54–61.

64. Sylwester, *The adolescent brain.*

65. Mary Helen Immordino-Yang and Antonio Damasio. "We feel, therefore we learn: the relevance of affective and social neuroscience to education." 2007. *The Jossey-Bass Reader on the Brain and Learning*. San Francisco, CA: Jossey-Bass Publishers, pp. 183–92.

66. W. E. Vine. *An expository dictionary of New Testament words*. 1966. Old Tappan, NJ: Fleming H. Revell Company. Vol. 3, pp. 21–24. See also H. E. Dana and Julius R. Mantey. *A manual grammar of the Greek new testament*. 1962. New York: The Macmillan Company.

67. W. E. Vine, *An expository dictionary of New Testament words*.

68. Ibid.

69. Nancy Brown. "Sexuality in the 21st century and beyond: Adolescents' behavior and beliefs." 2005. *Stanford University Palo Alto Medical Foundation*. Retrieved from www.pamf.org/teen/abc/sex/ethicalsex.html. Cf. C. S. Lewis, *The Four Loves*. 1960. New York: Harcourt, Brace, Jovanovich Publishers, passim, pp. 53–163.

70. Lewis, *The four loves*.

71. Deborah Stipek. "Relationships matter." March 2006. *Educational Leadership* 64(1): 46–49.

72. K. Shultz. *Listening: A framework for teaching across differences*. 2003. New York: Teachers College Press, p. 104.

73. D. V. Herman and M. Marlowe. "Modeling meaning in life: The teacher as servant leader." 2005. *Reclaiming Children and Youth* 14(3): 175–78.

74. V. Ruus et al., "Students' well-being, coping, academic success, and school climate." *School* 2007. *Behavior and Personality* 35(7): 919–36. Cf. Edward F. DeRoche and Mary M. Williams. *Character education: A guide for school administrators*. 2001. Lanham, MD: Scarecrow Press, pp. 51–58.

Chapter 2

Technology, Temptation, and Choices

Temptation cannot exist without the concurrence of inclination and opportunity.

—E. H. Chapin, *Living Words*

Who can forget the infamous 1990s criminal case of convicted rapist Mary Kay Letourneau and her Seattle elementary-school student Vili Fualaau? The Letourneau case broke just prior to the communication technology's boom. The technological ability to reach people instantly and anonymously changed the landscape of connectivity. What opportunities does this provide for today's teachers who possess the motivation and pursuit exhibited by Letourneau?

The fact is that sexual predators do not require advanced technologies and social networking to gain access to their prey but will use whatever means are available to them.[1] Letourneau had a direct access to her victim because she saw him every day as she and her student used more traditional handwritten notes and letters to communicate with her victim. This eventually proved to be her undoing, as documented in a television biography depicting her story.

As a result of her access, she was able to take sixth-grade student Vili Fualaau under her wing and subsequently groom him, by focusing on his artistic talents. In so doing, she had already crossed a moral line as a teacher. He spent time at her house, and she encouraged a friendship between him and her oldest child, Steve, who was only a year younger than Fualaau.

In June 1996, she began a sexual relationship with the thirteen-year-old, a relationship that Fualaau would later say he welcomed. The relationship came crashing to a halt in February 1997, when Steve Letourneau found love letters that his wife had written to Fualaau. Later that month, one of Steve's relatives reported the affair to officials at Shorewood Elementary. The police were notified, and Letourneau (who at the time was pregnant with Fualaau's child) was arrested and charged with statutory rape.[2]

Letourneau's access to the young student had begun at school, with regular contact in the classroom. Then it grew into spending time together away from school. Her predatory motivation drove her to pursue his affections, and she proved relentless in this pursuit.

Teachers who invite their students to their homes on a regular basis form relationships with them outside of the profession and communicate with notes and cards are sending troubling signals. These signals were somehow missed along the way, in Letourneau's case. In the years since the Letourneau case, communication access points have multiplied exponentially, and predators have found new ways to target victims.

In an article addressing sexual predators' use of technological advancements, journalist Kristen Doerschner writes that "before Internet and cellphone technology, most predators stayed close to home. The only way they could contact a victim was in person. Now, through such sites as Facebook, predators can look for potential victims who either fit a specific profile or who simply seize upon an opportunity."[3] Letourneau took advantage of the professional platform and of the students entrusted to her. The bottom line is that something went awry with Letourneau's moral compass when she felt her desires were more important than her mission as a teacher and her responsibilities to her family. She eventually left her family and sought out an elementary-school child as her soulmate. She persisted even after her arrest and imprisonment.

Thanks in large measure to the Letourneau case, more attention began to be paid to teacher-student relationships. But attention drawn to matters such as these is not enough. It is reactive and not proactive. The emergence of new technologies only enhances the possibilities of regular contacts between students and teachers outside of the classroom. Without proper guidance and moral boundaries, the problems will only continue to worsen.

The reality today is that "technology plays [a] role in inappropriate student-teacher relationships,"[4] and more and more teachers are blurring the lines of what are appropriate relationships between them.

TEACHER-SEX RELATIONSHIPS ARE HAPPENING MORE OFTEN

To be fair, the following questions must be asked as to whether (1) teacher-student sexual relationships are actually occurring more often today, (2) they are just being reported more often, or (3) the laws are stricter today than in years past, having revised what was allowable culturally in decades past?

Times have changed and a vast number of studies are relevant to teacher-student relationships, pertaining to (1) learning outcomes and student-classroom achievement, including high-school exit exams and standardized testing;[5] (2) increased literacy scores;[6] (3) teacher stress; (4) self-efficacy; (5) classroom management; and (6) student motivation.[7] But they have not adapted to the modern problems of teachers sexually abusing students.

Meta-analyses on teacher-student relationships focus mostly on what we already know: Teachers have tremendous impact on student learning and achievement, both positively and negatively. In his article covering twenty years of research on the subject, Theo Wubbels says that "the research examines teaching from an interpersonal perspective using a communicative systems approach and proposes a model to describe teacher-student relationships in terms of teacher behavior."[8]

An older British study asked "whether students' misbehavior had been consistently linked to teachers' reports of stress."[9] The authors speculate as to whether or not "teacher stress, negative affect, and self-efficacy predict the quality of student-teacher relationships."[10] The obvious answer was that teacher stress affected the learning outcomes of students in elementary classrooms.

To reiterate, there is no secret that the training of classroom teachers has changed over the past few decades. Laws are often revised in order to force teachers into one form of compliance or another. Yet laws are not enough. What is missing from the training of teachers is correlated to what is missing from the bulk of emerging education research.

Greater attention needs to be focused upon appropriate and inappropriate relationships between teachers and students, effective ways to develop boundaries, and the role that technology plays in forming and growing relationships between the two. Practically, if the law is the boundary, then teachers must be instructed on what behaviors are acceptable and what boundaries are necessary in healthy social and academic environments. Information is the key and ignorance is unacceptable.

REDISCOVERING THE TEACHER

In America's culture of sex, a by-product is sexual expression and gender identity. Today's teachers are entering classrooms with less assurance of their own professional identities but with heightened states of political correctness. Student identities have taken precedence and teachers are left uncertain how this affects teaching and learning. If students are uncertain as to who they are, how can they be certain of the ways they can learn? Teachers are caught with hearing one voice that asserts all brains are similar, and emotions are the key to learning. Another voice tells them that gender and sexuality are critical differences, beginning in the womb,[11] for subsequent learning styles, and science and biology always win in the end.

In some ways, the American education system is both a perpetrator and a victim. It has perpetrated social ideas that have teachers questioning their passion and moral purpose. It is also a victim, pushing agenda and programs that have very little to do with academic outcomes.

Teacher Identity

The idea of *teacher identity* being addressed here pertains to authority and profession and is not a descriptor of personal morality or sexuality. However, political correctness has now corralled the language of the classroom, and teachers must genuflect to the gender warriors or suffer serious career consequences. Education was not always like this.

For decades, teachers had been told that they were the most important persons in the classrooms. Unfortunately, this is no longer the case. Teacher wellness programs have arisen as a response to the changes in the American education system, which should reveal much about the state of the system. The psychological and physical impacts upon teachers being given the title of teacher, but allowed only to facilitate in kindness, have taken their toll. The notion of unwell teachers in classrooms across the nation does not present the healthiest of images of a workforce. Neither does the image present security for the system as a whole.

The teacher needs to be rediscovered as the professional in the classroom so as to better serve the students. A direct consequence of the confusion over much of teacher identity is the blurring of lines of respect for authority. In some cases, teachers are mere objects to the students. As a result, the reputations of teachers are afterthoughts among many students in classrooms today. Teachers, then, have little recourse, which is probably why so many of them seek to be friends with students. Students' friends receive more respect. Nevertheless, any relationships that develop without healthy foundations and clear moral lines are relationships headed for trouble.

TECHNOLOGY AND CHOICES

Modern technology allows ordinary people to cross paths quickly and on a regular basis. The same technology allows people to learn more about others from what is posted online and even help to cultivate relationships. Commercials abound on cable television, advertising websites that proclaim to have helped people find the loves of their lives or perfect dating partners.

Technology brings with it many choices. The ways in which these choices play out, and how the new medium is incorporated into culture, inform the society as a whole. Communication technologies have enabled relationships to be formed in ways that are a natural fit for teenage brains and their emotional impulses. Advertisers and marketers understand this quite well. Companies create applications for cell phones to capture impulses. Each company forms a type of digital communication in an effort to create an ongoing relationship with the app user. However, businesses are not alone in understanding teenagers and their technology.

Purveyors of sex understand this medium as well. This is one of the downsides to the new digital communications paradigm. Those who encourage inappropriate relationships with our teenagers are also aware of the technological possibilities that can be exploited. There is an old adage that *impulsivity and temptation have the same parent.* Certainly, one would be hard-pressed to find a more visible nexus of impulsivity and temptation than in the actions of some teenagers.

Proximity and location are no longer prohibitions to relationships. If there is communication service available, there are possibilities. People can send text messages to cell phones, share images and videos, post messages online, read and write e-mail, connect with a person on a voice call, combine all of those into a conference call, or maintain a cam audience.

Technology goes wherever we go and the rapid advancements in communication technologies have also blurred lines once deemed clearly marked between the professional and the personal. New technologies have softened some of the edges of traditional American cultural and moral customs, and these new horizons offer tempting choices for teachers and students.

Failed Policy

Whether in Texas, Florida, Idaho, or California, the story is always the same. Just walking the hallways of schools, or entering the student restrooms, observers will notice two behaviors. Despite laws and restrictions, many students are on their smartphones and some students are vaping.[12] Cell phone technology has brought with it a bevy of choices, and most people choose communication and other things over compliance with law or school policy.

As an example of the frustration of smartphones, several teachers at three large high schools in southern California gave up trying to enforce such bans altogether. Administrators all take the same ineffectual approach to addressing the problem: "Here is the district's cell phone policy, and it is to be supported on campus." It is time to admit that cell phone policies have failed and update the policies.[13]

Students think their cell phones are private property and that they can do whatever they wish with them at school. States like New York have tough bans on student technologies on campus. However, banning cell phones and music devices does very little to change student behaviors and mindsets.[14] Parents now expect to reach their child at any point throughout the school day.

Ubiquitous and Smart

Recent estimates indicate that approximately 95 percent of teenage students now "have access to a smartphone, a 22 percent increase since . . . 2015."[15] Students of all ages can take photographs or videos in restrooms or can violate test security by forwarding photographs sent to them by others. Secret videos have captured everything from sixty-second fights to teacher rants, to sex in restrooms. Through cell phones, students can plan flash mobs, start fights, bully others, or even cultivate rumors that persist throughout the course of an entire year. Students also use their phones to communicate with willing teachers in off-hours.

Society is becoming more litigious each year. Teachers and schools are rapidly approaching a time when they will be held legally responsible for what technological transmissions occur within their classrooms and on their campuses. It will no longer be enough to say that there is a policy in place concerning cell phone use. When a major incident occurs, the first question that will be asked will be about the nonenforcement of the district's cell phone policy. However, teachers must be kept up to date with their state's privacy laws as they pertain to their students.

Teachers must be aware that students send sexual comments about them to their friends in the class and that these comments circulate around the school. Also, teachers should know how they are talked about on social media. Nevertheless, let the record show that teachers are not the only school employees who have problems in the area of relationships with teenagers. For example, twenty-three-year-old former youth hockey coach Zachary Meints was arrested and charged in Boulder, Colorado, for sending *thousands* of sexual texts and Facebook messages to minors, asking them for naked photos and encouraging "masturbation races." He pleaded guilty to Internet sex exploitation.[16]

Unfortunately, cases like these are not isolated to extremes any longer. Another example of messages shared resulted in the suicide of a gay Tennessee teenager. The teenager was sending sexually explicit messages to another male classmate on SnapChat and Instagram. He trusted people and hoped that his posts would not be used against him. He was wrong. Two other students got hold of these posts and shared them online to embarrass the sixteen-year-old Channing Smith. Smith shot himself over the embarrassment it caused him at school. His actions of posting and trusting were mistakes.[17]

The actions of the boys violated trust. The lesson learned here is that it is a mistake to think that anything sexual involving teenagers is sacred. It is a mistake to post sexually explicit photos and messages. Teachers who trust that students will keep their trysts secret are sorely mistaken. Unfortunately, the freedom people feel when posting explicit sexual messages online is a by-product of America's sex culture. In Smith's case, it led to the loss of this gifted and talented young man.[18]

Not long ago cell phones were just an isolated annoyance, ringing occasionally during class time. Today, the issue is keeping students from taking pictures, recording videos, and sending texts during class. One clandestine video can ruin a career or lead to serious allegations that will hang over a person forever. Emily Salazar's story is a good example.

The former high-school teacher and mentor ran an adult porn website where her sexual activities were recorded by her husband and uploaded to their site. Students from the school found out and shared her videos around the school and to the other high schools in the district. Salazar was placed on paid administrative leave and she later resigned from her position. She currently remains credentialed to teach and serves as a fitness instruction, since it was demonstrated that no crimes were committed.[19]

TEMPTATION AND STIMULATION

Easier access to people through technology brings with it the possibility of elevated emotions and the possibility of an aroused state between those who communicate. Often, the imagination must come into play to interpret online posts and text messages. To what extent does regular communication stimulate the brain? Adults who spend an inordinate amount of personal time communicating through technology tend to communicate in a more relaxed manner. Yet comments may be posted that they would never consider sharing in face-to-face communication. There is a similar norm with students as they communicate with each other.

For example, online bullying can create such a high level of emotional stimulation and its effects could cause others emotional distress or even result in self-harm. Sadly, it is becoming more commonplace to hear that online comments had become parts of the reasons student had taken their own lives. Sadly, bullying is not only affecting students.

Adults have realized that with certain anonymity they are able to punish people, sully reputations, and cause unrest. There is a certain pseudo-confidence of impunity that accompanies faceless communication, and ages and gender are not barriers to these practices. Fortunately, social networking sites are making it more difficult to remain anonymous. But there is a long way to go to raise the level of accountability to one of greater transparency.

Teenagers face an onslaught of stimuli that arouse them emotionally and physically. Video games, social events, communication with friends, and even food all "fire up" the average teenager's brain. Another flashpoint for arousal pertains to sex, which now increasingly infiltrates teenage culture via the smartphone. Porn addiction is real[20] and likely has something to do with the increase of teacher-student sexual relationships. Technologies on the go mean that stimuli are also on the go, continually bombarding students' brains. These same stimuli also creep into the minds of adults.

Recent data from the American Addiction Centers[21] are sobering. Nine out of ten boys are exposed to porn before age eighteen, and six out of ten girls are exposed to porn before the same age.[22] The research into teenage exposure to pornography indicates that teenagers "exposed to sexually explicit websites are more likely to be promiscuous and more likely to have used alcohol or other intoxicating substances during their last sexual encounter."[23] In many of the cases involving teachers and students having sex, recording their behaviors, intoxicants are often found to be involved.

SEXUAL TEMPTATIONS IN TODAY'S SEX CULTURE

Temptations are not evil. But what people do when temptation arises can result in temporary pleasure as well as cause serious emotional and physical problems. There are six basic sexual temptations underlying America's sex culture, each of which can be a flashpoint for students' eventual involvement in sexual activity. These are found in table 2.1 and are addressed in the explanations that follow. While teachers and students are both affected by sexual temptation within the classroom, teachers must take care to reject certain temptation and make sure never to entertain the slightest of sexual imaginations involving students.

Sexual Identity

Sexual expression of the past is now aligned with sexual identity, defining who people are over what they do. The first sexual temptation involves changing the standard for what refers to be *normal*. The term *normal* has been given many definitions over the years and continues to evolve even with Gen Z. Today. A new definition is aligned with a new set of subjective norms, particularly regarding sexual orientation, feelings, and expressions. Culture has shifted so that it is now possible to feel one's way into a change of sexual identity and gender.

Table 2.1   Six Sexual Temptations Affecting Students in America's Sex Culture

1. *Sexual Identity:*
Sexual expression of the past is now aligned with sexual identity, defining who we are over what we do.

2. *Sexual Expression:*
Expression of sexual identity in class draws attention to oneself.

3. *Pornography:*
Pornography and sexual experimentation attract students for sexual exploitation and are concerns toward increased levels of addiction.

4. *Sexual Boldness:*
Students use bold approaches to express their sexual identity in language, photographs, and practice, as a means to exaggerate their sexuality. This boldness is sometimes expressed in the direction of teachers.

5. *Sexual Language:*
Students post specific sexual language on public Internet forums toward teachers and friends, and these are shared with friends.

6. *Sexual Fantasy:*
Sexual identity combined with technology, pornography, and youthful imagination may give birth to a new cultural phenomenon—*the emerging teenage/student sexual predator.*

People are known more today by their cultural labels or by their personal feelings about their identities rather than by a generalized corporate label, such as Americans or humans. Everyone seems to have a hyphenation, which tends to focus on differences. Therefore, part of the problem today in schools is the notion that one's sexual identity needs to be owned and expressed, over a larger corporate label. Students' identities are now defined by what students call themselves.

Ironically, a major problem with this thinking involves a biological reality. Teenagers are not mature enough to know the extent of their beliefs or actions. They are not wired up enough to understand that owning a cultural label may not be such a good thing in the long run. Connections with groups and individuals via the Internet help to feed this temptation toward definition and self-expression during the experimental teenage years. If a student has suddenly changed his behaviors and makes outrageous claims about himself, or herself, a parent should check the online sites and the groups with which there are regular communications. Chances are the influences are present on the student's smart devices.

Sexual Expression

The second sexual temptation involves students' *expressions* of their sexual identities. These are the actions they take based on feelings of identities they claim. Teachers today contend with various expressions of student sexuality. Some students are activism-oriented and boisterous about their sexual relationships. Teachers are threatened that speaking out against sexual expression of one group or another is hateful. Sexual expression on campus has no place, as it interferes with the focus of the school. Schools do not exist for self-expression, despite what is being allowed by some. This goes for any and all sexual expressions. They certainly do not exist for any one person's or group's sexuality.

Beware the Predators

National and state databases of sexual predators are found online, thanks to Megan's Law.[24] The U.S. Department of Justice's website is an online portal for tracking registered offenders who may also be legally classified as sexual predators.[25] Anywhere that children assemble is a place restricted to sex offenders. Just contacting children via the Internet is enough to weigh against a person classified as a sexual predator.[26]

Sex trafficking of children is an enormous problem, and teenagers do not escape the attention of predators. In some ways, confusion of identity, self-expression, political correctness, at-risk youth, and technology are woven together by criminal minds, placing our nation's students at greater risk.

The British newspaper *The Derby Telegraph* warns its readers that "any youngster with a mobile phone or Web access is at risk of [sexual] exploitation." In the article, Mandy MacDonald, child protective manager for the city of Derby, goes on to say that "it's very easy for someone to manipulate [the] adolescent phase, where the young people are so naive and feel they are invincible. They are very impulsive. They think emotionally rather than reasoning."[27] Thus, there comes great temptation with most technological advances.

Sex procurement is no exception. In an attempt to curb some of the Internet sex-trafficking, President Trump signed into law the 2018 Fight Online Sex Trafficking Act, which was responsible for shutting down some sex-related Internet sites and sex-related advertising site, such as Backpage.[28]

Pornography

A third sexual temptation exists because of the easy access today's teenagers and adults have to pornography. Porn hurts teenagers for many reasons,[29] including (1) breaking down moral barriers to early sex and possible pregnancy, (2) disorienting and skewing teenagers' thinking about relational and consensual sex, (3) the risking of depression and feelings of insecurity, and (4) lowering self-esteem by setting up unrealistic expectations.

Sex has gone mainstream, digitally. It can be brought to immediate attention with the click of a mouse and shared with a simple *send*. The Internet allows millions of users daily access to pornography through computers, cell phones, and other devices.

Ogi Ogas and Sai Gaddam, coauthors of *A billion wicked thoughts*, were interviewed by *Forbes* contributing columnist Julie Ruvolo, where they drew the following conclusions:

> In 2010, out of the million most popular websites in the world, 42,337 were sex-related sites. That's about 4 percent of sites. From July 2009 to July 2010, about 13 percent of Web searches were for erotic content. You could also look at the number of 'adult sites' that are blocked by various parental filtering software programs—for example, CYBERsitter claims to block 2.5 million adult Web sites.[30]

Since that time, the number of Internet porn sites and porn consumers has grown. The cybersecurity company Webroot has provided the public with the following tabulations from some of the "most credible statistics available today on internet pornography."[31] Table 2.2 is a condensed version of these statistics.

Porn Sport

Again, beware sexual predators. These adults prey on women and men and pay them to record their actions in permanent retrieval systems. College campuses are especially targeted. Female students are paid a sum of money to perform sex acts, and coed escorts are paid to participate in fraternity and college sex parties. Interest at a younger age in posting sexually suggestive photos correlates to eventual higher-risk behavior during early adulthood. Temptations to both advertise and secure *flesh for sale* have taken hold and have placed another stone along the path of participation in multiple pornographic settings.

Table 2.2   Access to Internet Pornography

Every Second	• 28,258 users watching Internet porn • $3,075.64 is being spent on Internet porn
Every Day	• 37 porn videos are created in the United States • 2.5 billion e-mails containing porn are sent or forwarded • 68 million search queries related to porn are generated • 116,000 queries related to child porn are received
Affects upon Americans	• Estimated 200,000 Americans are classified as porn addicts • 40 million Americans regularly visit porn sites • 35 percent of all downloads are porn-related • 34 percent of Internet users have experienced unwanted porn through ads, pop-ups, or misdirected links or e-mails. • One-third of Internet porn viewers are women

Female teens "are far more likely than male teens to post personal photos or videos of themselves online."[32] This is evident in our schools, both public and private. Some teachers and students send around photos and videos of themselves through real-time communications by video cam and cell phone livestreaming and recorded videos.

Sexual experimentation, which now includes "sexting," is viewed by youths as a techno-recreational sport. "Seventy-one percent of teen girls and 67 percent of boys who sent or posted sexually suggestive content say they sent it to a boyfriend or girlfriend."[33] Sexual exploitation of students in schools involves minors. Sadly, teenagers are sometimes all-too-willing participants in this exploitation, another indicator of the impulsivity and immaturity that often accompany this age group.

Last, given both the increase in teenage usage of porn and the dramatic increase in adult female porn usage, there should be additional research into two areas: (1) whether the increase of female teachers arrested and Internet porn usage had any significant correlation, and (2) whether moral boundaries of teenagers to become involved in sex with their teachers had been affected by usage of porn over time. Hence, the coining of the term *porn sport*.

Sexual Boldness

The fourth sexual temptation deals with boldness in flaunting sexuality. Teenagers know sexuality is powerful. Students today are less shy about their approach to adults than in the past.

Many students feel as if they can talk to their teachers about anything and tease them in ways that ought to be reserved for friends. Frankly, teachers are skilled at opening up teenagers' minds and hearts and are often willing to reach into their lives. However, are teachers expert at knowing how to deal with students once these teens are open?

Professional development and straightforward conversations can help. Crossing lines and then scaling back afterward sends mixed messages. Teenagers view teachers as buddies in some cases and often with relational impunity. Teachers do not have the same luxury and they should not have the same attitude as their students, on this issue.[34]

Another part of teenage sexual boldness comes from watching adults play at their sexuality and command respect from the elite within culture for their playfulness. For example, this is found in the rise of the cougar and cub phenomenon, portraying *mature* women as sex-starved and needing to appease their sexual appetites with much younger men.

Programs like *Sex and the City* (1998–2004) celebrated what is known as the *cougar phenomenon* weekly. Today's younger teachers were some of the viewers of programs such as this. There are fine lines between entertainment and encouragement. Though *Sex and the City* writer Candace Bushnell rejects the notion that the show emboldened women to seek younger sex partners, not everyone was convinced.[35] Some report that the "cougar" approach is apparently quite appealing to teenagers and might be a leading cause of young female teachers—even those married—seeking even younger males as sex partners.[36]

As an example of the debate over the cougar phenomenon, a local community was stunned to learn that a forty-something parent had had sex with her daughter's eighteen-year-old boyfriend. The teenager, a recent high-school graduate, was her victim because she said *it made her feel sexy*. This story was related to the author by the woman's teenage daughter. The daughter was appalled, but her boyfriend referred to the experience as *cool* and *no big deal*.

Online magazines such as *Cosmopolitan* and *Teen Vogue* often extol the pleasures of sex from all possible angles. Girls and young women gain insights on sexual practices. Fantasy sites abound for teens who fantasize having sex with their moms, or dads, as well as the moms and dads of their friends. This phenomenon is increasing to alarming levels in our nation, and Internet porn is replete with videos depicting these very fantasies.[37]

Television programs and movies celebrate sexual boldness in many ways. One way it is celebrated is playing up relationships that have age differences. Hollywood also uses the coupling of power and fantasy to perpetuate the boldness. Hollywood stars, such as Tom Cruise and Katie Holmes, as well as Demi Moore and Ashton Kutcher, gained notoriety and headlines for their undying love that spans the age differences, only to be found again in the headlines when they broke up a few years later.

Actor Charlie Sheen's notorious drug-fueled sex parties were all students seemed talking about for months. He described his antics as *winning*, the modifier which became quite an annoying fad in some classrooms. Teenagers are susceptible to imitating adults' sexual antics.

Games and movies have even been created with the goal to see how many people they can have sex or lose their virginity before they graduate high school. Even worse, there are new studies indicating that some boys are having sex before age thirteen. This means that America's sex culture has affected so many younger children.[38]

Then came the Hollywood fallout, with Bill Cosby, Harvey Weinstein, Jeffrey Epstein, and so many more being accused of or arrested for sexual misconduct.[39] All were sexual predators, having sex with young women. But in the case of Epstein, his pedophilia-driven lusts were fulfilled by sex with young girls.[40] From grooming of Hollywood children[41] to sex trafficking,[42] to sexual *quid pro quo* with models,[43] young girls and young woman were lured into sex by physical threats, employment promises, money, drugs, and alcohol. Experts fear that schools are powerless to stop it from happening in their midst.[44] Consider that these occurrences were not kept highly secretive.

If culture shapers are to be believed, then everyone is now sexy at all ages. This is good news to pedophiles whose sexual tastes are usually prepubescent children. Pedophilia is quickly becoming an acceptable sexual orientation, both legally and within the bounds of America's excessive sex culture. Young girls and teenagers from all over the world are trafficked to the United States for one purpose. That purpose is for people to pay for sex with them.

Those who shape culture would have us believe that earlier sexual experiences are now a national preoccupation and national pastime.[45] Teenagers who have bought into this philosophy are left devastated after their attempts to secure the feelings in real life that are often fictionalized online. American culture is producing sex addicts in growing numbers,[46] and the trend is headed in the most disturbing of directions.

Sexual Language

Fifth, sexual language is a powerful tool, given the uniqueness of teenagers. Sexual empowerment is found in the words and images they use to describe each other. Words can elevate someone's sexual stature, or they can bring someone to ruin in a flash. Recently, a group of male students said they wouldn't mind having sex with a younger female teacher, describing what they would do if they had the chance. After having stepped into the middle of that conversation, one look caused that conversation to change course. In a moment, their passion dissipated, and remorse was expressed. Their sexual empowerment had lost to an authority with a different empowerment and one which clearly demonstrated that students had crossed a line.

Countless teachers have been referred to as "hot" or "sexy." Descriptions of sexual acts that the students would enjoy performing on teachers have been posted online for the world to see.[47] Whether teasing or not, students commenting about sex acts with teachers is a form of sexual harassment. In some cases this harassment is born of a fictional fantasy. But whatever the fantasy, such *teasing* can ruin a person's reputation and even result in the loss of a career. Some students think that all that is required to negate such comments is to follow the negative comments with an emoticon or animation. Students may play with their sexuality, but words are indeed currency.

Sexual Fantasy

Finally, there is power in sexual fantasy, which the teenage mind mixes with reality. Fantasy includes words, images, and emotions stirred with idealism and imagination. Technology enhances these fantasies, whether virtually or by personal contact with people. Technology allows deliberate visual and audio fixation and thereby increases the opportunity to dwell on something as if it's real. As an example of this, a male student who thinks his young female math teacher is *hot* and shares this with his friends is likely to get encouraging responses from his peers about things he ought to do with this teacher. What is the reality, and what is the fantasy?

The prolonged mental entertainment of fantasies sometimes allows them to take on lives of their own. Sexual fantasy is not assigned only to teenagers. Adults also use fantasy to manipulate the minds of others, which is why fantasy narratives are so appealing. When sexual fantasy orchestrated by adults reaches into the reality of teenagers, there can be serious problems. Some teenagers actually believe the images painted for them by culture shapers. One example of this is the celebration of sexual orientations and gender fluidity.

Students—especially male students—are well aware of sexual-escort sites and other sex sites. Ashley Madison's site is for married men and women looking to cheat on their spouses. Madison's site is now even commercially advertised on cable television. Literally, anything and everything sexually can be found on the Internet for a price or even for free.[48]

It does not take an extensive search online to find women and men willing to engage in sexual activities with younger children and teenagers. There is an entire underground online network of child sexual predators, one in which Americans are involved.[49] For example, adult teenage girls can be found seeking out *daddy figures* on the Internet, teasing supposedly older men to be their *sugar daddies*, caring for their desires in exchange for sexual pleasure. The sad reality is that female teachers are today also seeking the same, under the guise of supplementing their salaries.[50]

Certain slightly built young gay men are known as *twinks* and offer their services to men attracted to boyish young adults. Older, hairy men, known as *bears*, seek out sex with *cubs*, the term for younger gay men. Women seek males and they nickname *cubs*, or women seek females, which they call *kittens*, a term for younger lesbian lovers. There are pedophile groups, such as the North American Man/Boy Love Association (NAMBLA),[51] which promotes adult relationships between children and adult pedophiles, proving again just how depraved America's sex culture has become.

Whatever the homosexual or heterosexual temptations found in the fantasies of students and adults, the fulfillment of the fantasies is readily available in America. Though many of these relationships begin in the mind as sexual fantasies, in the end the issue here is that the sex is real. Teachers would be amazed at how many students have played out their sexual fantasies about them[52] and would be more than willing participants.

So what does it take for a teenager with no sexual experience to move into a very risky behavioral mode? Igra and Irwin "describe that risk-taking behaviors usually display a 'developmental trajectory,' increasing as a teenager grows older. For example, rates of sexuality, reckless vehicle use, and substance use increase with age."[53] Why do teenagers view teachers as conquests? Is there a new teenage phenomenon rising from the current digital porn-saturated, free-wheeling sex culture? Could it be that with the growth of sexual encounters of students with adults, and the various addictions described within this chapter, schools will soon witness the onset of a generation of new sexual offenders, *the teenage sexual predator, where teachers are the actual victims*?

CULTURAL VOICES AFFECTING RELATIONSHIPS

Presently, technology has made it easy to publish rumors and glitzy half-truths and to make them come across as believable and attractive. Certain old-school seductions merely are repackaged in their presentation to emerging generations. Generation Z is not exempt from these. Teachers who have been around for some time understand that there really is nothing new about these seductions. What is new, though, are opportunities, access points, and flashy-digital sexy packaging. King Solomon, who reigned ca.970 to 931 BC, uttered words of wisdom so familiar to many readers of the Bible:

> All streams flow into the sea, yet the sea is never full. To the place the streams come from, there they return again. All things are wearisome, more than one can say. The eye never has enough of seeing, nor the ear its fill of hearing. What has been will be again, what has been done will be done again; there is nothing new under the sun. Is there anything of which one can say, "Look! This is something new?" It was here already, long ago; it was here before our time. No one remembers the former generations, and even those yet to come will not be remembered by those who follow them.[54]

Solomon was correct in his assessment of life. He tried it all and came up woefully empty as a person. He aspired to find his identity in every conceivable vice available to a monarch. To the extent that technology speeds up the opportunities to experiment, the results and consequences of the experimentation are just as exhausting for people who are chasing their own vanities.

Today's teenagers have been sexualized, and their senses are overloaded. Humans are sometimes reduced to objects of lust, torture, and abuse. This reduction is even more heinous when younger children are the victims. Recently, one of the largest busts of child pornography was made. Let the readers beware of the graphic nature found in the summarized text below:

[Forty-three] men have been arrested over the past two years in a horrific, far-flung child porn network. . . . Authorities have identified more than 140 young victims so far and say there is no end in sight as they pore through hundreds of thousands of images found on the suspects' computers. Photos and online chats found on computers owned by [Robert] Diduca and [Robert] Mikelsons led to more than three dozen other suspects in seven countries. . . . The oldest victim . . . was four, the youngest just nineteen days old. Massachusetts U.S. Attorney Carmen Ortiz said the demand for photos of sexual assaults of young children, including babies and toddlers, has increased sharply in recent years. Diduca pleaded guilty to child-porn and sexual-exploitation charges and was sentenced to eighteen years in prison. His lawyer said Diduca was sexually abused as a child by a Boy Scout leader. Mikelsons also received an eighteen-year sentence, followed by indefinite psychiatric commitment, after confessing to sexually abusing more than eighty children. The horror did not let up after the Mikelsons case . . . authorities arrested Michael Arnett of Roeland Park, Kan., after finding pornographic photos he allegedly produced. What they found on Arnett's computer was unlike anything some of the investigators had ever come across: long, graphic, online chats about his desire to abduct, kill and eat children.[55]

The Voices of Neutrality

It has been argued that technology is neutral. Everyone agrees that molded plastics, thin wires, computer chips, and circuit boards have no morality. As with all things neutral, one must always consider the motivation behind an invention and the inventor's original vision for the technology. The moment humans use an invention, it becomes purposeful. We can see this from the example of any child pornography bust, where it was revealed that criminals had used technology for evil, but law enforcement had used the same technology for good. Teenagers need to be made aware that their device usage comes with consequences if they choose to use it wrongly. Teachers also need this understanding.

In terms of the Internet, the worldwide web only became a reality for the public between 1993 and 1995. However, what we now know as the Internet had its fledgling beginnings during the Cold War period. It was created for a purpose and was initially labeled ARPANET, used by the Department of Defense and other government agencies subsequent to the 1960s. The authors of "Brief history of the internet"[56] illustrate the importance of this technological advancement.

The Internet has "revolutionized the computer and communications world like nothing before. The . . . telegraph, telephone, radio, and computer set the stage for this unprecedented integration of capabilities. The Internet is at once a worldwide broadcasting capability, a mechanism for information dissemination, and a medium for collaboration and interaction between individuals and their computers without regard for geographic location."[57]

Currently, the Internet is used to gather campaign donations and assist in billing transactions and banking. Stock trading is done online. E-mail is still a significant type of communication in businesses and education.

The Internet has revolutionized how people relate to each other and has made to the road to publishing research much smoother. Hearkening to the words of Michael Fullan, one wonders whether scratching a good teacher who uses today's communication technologies wisely and appropriately becomes part of a new paradigm of moral purpose.[58]

Who can forget the sights and sounds of the Arab Spring of 2012? We revel in Skype, Zoom, GoToMeeting, SnapChat, Facebook, WhatsApp, Instagram, TikTok, and Twitter as having become *virtual* corporate and household names. Technology has changed our lives. It was just a few decades ago that comic-book-loving children imagined a world with 1960s *Dick Tracy*—like watch a *Get Smart* shoe phone or a *James Bond* futuristic automobile.

Smartphones have surpassed the imaginations of the recent past. While many changes in technology have been notably wonderful additions to modern culture, some have not been so kind. Technology can bring out the best and worst in our character.

The Voices of Availability

Social networking sites provide voices for all seeking an audience. Information sites and search engines take us to worlds of data on nearly any topic in the universe. Emergency notifications and rapid life-saving responses are available in minutes or even seconds. People can be in touch with others in foreign countries right from their automobiles or living rooms. Websites are even set up for people to make quick selections and purchases of goods and services—with same day delivery. America's sex culture has provided convenience too. Some of our teenagers will have sex this year for the first times in their lives, and it just might be with an adult.

There will no doubt be stories about how girls dumped their boyfriends after discovering that they had used their smartphone cameras to record private acts or to immediately text their friends. Some young women will get pregnant, and their reputations will be sullied around school campuses. Others will drink, get drunk, or try drugs for the first times in their lives. All of these behaviors are made easier to come by as a result of technology. Groups can assemble quickly and impulsively. Followings online and *likes* have become motivation and incentive to become even more emboldened. In fact, some online platforms allow people to monetize their postings, if they reach certain viewership or *like* thresholds.

The Voices of the Mob

A *flash mob* is the gathering of hundreds or even thousands of people informed about an event via online messages. Blogger Tina Sieber writes that "flash mobs are an Internet phenomenon of the twenty-first century."[59] The short-lived Occupy Wall Street 2.0 movement of 2012 is an example of the use of technology to organize many people in a short period of time.[60] Technology has been credited with helping to orchestrate the fall of regimes in the Middle East[61] to violent robberies of dozens of pairs of jeans from clothing stores.[62] Over 90 percent of the crimes committed today by teenagers are committed in flash mobs. Violent assaults and arguments are captured by anyone standing around with a smartphone.

The ease of access and use of technology

> hasn't just made it easy to plan and organize events and tempting to take part in. It has allowed the thieves to off-load their loot. Technology has enable drug and sex traffickers easier access to customers. The online customers search from a plentiful supply that is offered, whether from drug dealers or from traffickers of child sex slaves.
>
> Given the sex culture that exists today, the chances that formerly trafficked children will be seated in one or more classrooms is a given. Even thieves have found that selling stolen goods has been simplified. A recent survey done by a leading retail-industry group shows that technology has led to a spike in organized crime, mostly as thieves find it easier to sell stolen goods online.[63]

CASE EXAMPLES

The following headlines of reported cases around the nation represent a small fraction of the overall allegations and arrests involving inappropriate and/or sexual relationships between teachers, school personnel, and students. The statistics are frightening.

Many of these arrests could have been avoided with a basic presentation of targeted professional development, including a focus on legalities and policy guidelines. As the readers examine the following cases, consider that professional development could have helped limit some of the poor choices and eventual crimes. Effective professional development would help in clearly stating (1) what appropriate relationships with students look like, (2) the boundaries between students and teachers, and (3) the ethics of using technology after-hours with students.

- "Former Fruitland High track coach charged with rape"[64]
- "Teacher accused of having sex with student allegedly had toddler present in home"[65]

- "Former Ohio teacher facing sex charges involving 28 first grade girls"[66]
- "Teacher, 51, accused of sexually abusing 14-year-old boy for months"[67]
- "Teacher, accused of having sex with teen 300 times"[68]
- "Des Moines teacher accused of offering sex to teenage student"[69]
- "Female teachers having sex, inappropriate relationships with students"[70]
- "Female New York teacher accused of having sex with student in motel"[71]
- "Biology teacher allegedly raped boy multiple times over summer break"[72]
- "Married Pennsylvania teachers sexually abused teen girl—wife wanted him to 'get it out of his system'"[73]
- "Former Arvada High School assistant principal arrested for alleged sexual relationship"[74]
- "Teacher accused of molesting elementary student was allowed to quietly retire"[75]
- "Head soccer coach accused of sex with minor"[76]
- "Former teacher allegedly had sex with 16-year-old student in school closet"[77]
- "Former Fresno middle school teacher sentenced to a year in jail for sex crimes with student"[78]
- "Bronx teacher who performed oral sex on 14-year-old gets 10 years' probation, avoids jail, keeps teaching certificate"[79]
- "Assistant cheerleading coach arrested for allegedly performing sexual acts on student, age 17"[80]
- "New Berlin schools, former teacher sued over 1980s sex abuse allegations"[81]
- "Former band teacher pleads no contest to sex acts with child under 14"[82]
- "Freedom High school teacher, Notre Dame standout charged with sex with minor"[83]
- "Jordan Baptist school teacher's alleged sex assault of students released in court, bond set at $750K"[84]
- "Louisiana elementary school teacher allegedly raped her 10-year-old student"[85]
- "Rhonda Eisenberg, teacher who gave birth to student's child, will be fired"[86]
- "Ex-school nurse admits to sex with teen after trying to bribe him with $2,000 car payment"[87]
- "Boxing coach arrested on suspicion of molesting teen boxer"[88]
- "Ex-Rowland elementary teacher gets 5 years for inappropriately touching 5 students"[89]
- "Ex-Arizona teacher sentenced to 20 years in prison for sex with student"[90]
- "Woman accused of raping teen with ex-husband"[91]
- "Texas substitute teacher fired after filming porn in classroom"[92]

- "Hayden elementary school teacher arrested for sex abuse of a minor charges"[93]
- "Middle school vice principal gets 3 years for sex act with teen girl"[94]
- "Teen molested by catholic school teacher gets record $8-million settlement from LA. Archdiocese"[95]

A WAKE-UP CALL

As parents are lobbied by children for more trust, adults find themselves increasingly more pressured by culture. Appropriate relationships with children begin at home. Teachers and parents should work together to ensure that students make the best and most wholesome choices possible for their lives and not allow the very tools and toys they own to become a source of moral compromise in their lives or the lives of their friends. Parents should always be the primary bulwark of protection for their children.

The following real-life scenarios emphasize the importance of dealing with today's children, as families are confronted with America's sex culture. Readers are encouraged to respond to the questions that coincide with each of the scenarios.

SCENARIO 1

Imagine that one day a fifth-grade member of your family begins spending significant time devising a plan with others to bully fellow student. This plan is posted online and you are alerted to this posting by another parent.

- Are you concerned? If so, at what level? Are students just doing what they always do?
- What steps, if any, would you take to end their plan?
- In what ways would your relationship with your child be impacted, both positively and negatively?
- What response should be given to the parent who notified others about the online posting?

SCENARIO 2

One day, after arriving home from your work, you discover one of your teenagers is missing. After phoning the police, you are informed that your daughter was possibly abducted by a registered sex offender. Following a detailed analysis of your daughter's computer, police discover that your teenager was entertaining a relationship with a person who had been pretending to be a lovesick *online buddy*. After a time, the man is apprehended at the location where he had planned to abduct your daughter. Fortunately, your daughter is returned safely to you.

- Why do you think your daughter left?
- What are your feelings about this incident?
- Is there anything you would do differently with your teenage daughter, after such an incident?
- What discussions would you now have with your teenage daughter about sexuality?
- What role did technology play in all parts of this scenario?

SCENARIO 3

A male teacher who coaches a team your son plays on begins making advances toward your sixteen-year-old son. You notice something odd between the coach and your son after one of his games. However, you let it go. Two weeks later, you read in the local newspaper that the coach is arrested for allegedly molesting some of his players. You find that your son and the coach were texting sexual comments to each other during evening hours, and now you must question your son.

- What conversations would you have with your son now that the coach has been arrested?
- How could you have handled the occurrence of the odd moment differently after one of your son's games?
- In what ways would your communication with your son change?
- What assistance would you need if you discovered your son was also a sexual victim of the coach?

SUMMARY

Teachers place greater attention on their relationships with students for a variety of reasons. The media pounces on scandals that involve teachers and students. The emergence of new technologies enhances the possibilities of contacts between teachers and students. The simple fact today is that technology plays several roles in the introduction of development of relationships between teachers and students. This same technology is also an avenue for inappropriate relationships between them.

There is great need for education-research institutions to study and analyze the impacts of teacher-student romantic and sexual relationships. Teachers are humans with real human needs. Modern technology allows ordinary people to cross paths quickly and, on a regular basis, to assist in meeting needs. The same technology allows people to learn more about others and even begin relationships. Proximity and location are no longer prohibitions to relationships.

The message is clear that students do not respect school cell phone policies, as a rule. Parents often support their children and contact them via text message and phone calls during school hours. Teachers battle this every day. The distractions are annoying and unprofessional.

Temptations are not evil. What people do when temptation presents itself could result in serious problems. Six sexual temptations that exist in today's teenage culture are (1) to convince people there is no "normal," (2) for students to express their sexual identities, (3) to easily access pornography, (4) to use sexual language-empowered words and images, (5) to build up or tear down someone's sexual stature and reputation, and (6) to engage in sexual fantasy. All of these are associated with the use of smartphone technology and computers.

Teachers and students experience sexual temptations within the classroom but to varying degrees. These temptations may carry over into off-hours and take root, as emotional connections almost always precede the physical relationships that develop. However, not all teachers and students are tempted to have sex with each other.

Social networking sites provide voices to all who seek an audience. Information sites and search engines provide us worlds of data on nearly any topic in the universe. Emergency notifications and rapid life-saving responses are available in mere seconds. People can be in touch with others, including sexual predators, in a matter of seconds.

Teacher training is vital in helping teachers to see the benefits of appropriate relationships with students, and the detriments of those which are inappropriate. Smart technology is not going away and must be managed ethically by teachers and students in this culture of sex that exists in America.

DISCUSSION QUESTIONS

1. In what ways are teenagers tempted today, and why does it appear easier to succumb to temptation today?

2. Why do you think more teachers are having sexual relationships with their teenage students?
3. What do you think is a good balanced school policy, in terms of relationship boundaries for teachers and students?
4. Does your district or school have an up-to-date and sensible acceptable-use technology policy for its teachers and students? Does it also apply to outside of school?
5. What are some cultural flashpoints of the chapter, and why might they be concerns for teachers?
6. How would you approach your own child if you were to discover that he or she has been viewing a great deal of pornography as well as sexting with much older friends?

NOTES

1. Ernest J. Zarra, III. *It should never happen here.* 1997. Grand Rapids, MI: Baker Book House, pp. 13–25.

2. "Mary Kay Letourneau: Biography." *Biography.com.* May 3, 2012. Retrieved from www.biography.com/people/mary-kay-letourneau-9542379.

3. Staff. "Technology allows sexual predators to operate differently." *Times Online.* April 17, 2011. Retrieved from www.timesonline.com/news/technology-allows-sexual-predators-to-operate-differently/article_05199b28-68b0-11e0-b4a4-001a4bcf6878.html.

4. Staff. "Technology plays role in inappropriate student-teacher relationships." *eSchool News.* June 28, 2011. Retrieved from www.eschoolnews.com/2011/06/28/technology-plays-role-in-inappropriate-student-teacher-relationships/.

5. Ruby Larson. "Teacher-student relationships and student achievement." *University of Nebraska—Omaha.* Retrieved from http://coe.unomaha.edu/moec/briefs/EDAD9550larson.pdf.

6. A. M. Klem and J. P. Connell. "Relationships matter: Linking teacher support to students." 2004. *Journal of School Health* 74(7): 262–73.

7. G. P. Montalvo, E. A. Mansfield, and R. B. Miller. "Liking or disliking the teacher: Student motivation, engagement, and achievement." 2007. *Evaluation and Research in Education* 20(3): 144–58. Retrieved from http://dx.doi.org/10.2167/eri406.0.

8. Staff. "Two decades of research on teacher-student relationships in class." 2005. *International Journal of Educational Research* 43(1–2): 6–24.

9. Isca Salzberger-Wittenberg, Gianna Henry, and Elsie Osborne. "The emotional experience of learning and teaching." 1984. *Journal of Child Psychotherapy* 10: 125.

10. Ibid., pp. 125–27.

11. Harry Pettit. "Women ARE born to be different as experts prove 'brain differences begin in the womb.'" *The Sun.* March 25, 2019. Retrieved from https://www.thesun.co.uk/tech/8711857/men-women-born-different-brain/.

12. Lisa Barone. "Banning social media doesn't work, education does." *Social Media*. May 5, 2010. Retrieved from http://smallbiztrends.com/2010/05/banning-social-media-doesn%E2%80%99t-work-education-does.html. Cf. Tom Andreesen and Cal Slemp. "Managing risk in a social media-driven society." *Protiviti*. 2001. Retrieved from www.protiviti.com/en-US/Documents/Insights/Managing-Risk-in-a-Social-Media-Driven-Society.pdf.

13. Staff. "Kern High School District Technology Plan: July 2010 to June 2013." *Kern High School District*. Retrieved www.khsd.k12.ca.us/Business/PDF/KHSD%20-%20Technology%20Plan-10-13.pdf.

14. Staff. "School cell phone ban causes uproar." *CBS News*. February 11, 2009. Retrieved from www.cbsnews.com/2100-201_162-1616330.html.

15. Monica Anderson and JingJing Jiang. "Teens, social media & technology 2018." *Pew Research Center*. May 31, 2018. Retrieved from https://www.pewinternet.org/2018/05/31/teens-social-media-technology-2018/.

16. Zachary Meints. "Youth hockey coach that sent boys sexual texts, pleads guilty to internet sex exploitation." *Huffington Post*. May 30, 2012. Retrieved from www.huffingtonpost.com/2012/05/30/zachary-meints-former-bou_n_1557128.html.

17. K. C. Baker. "Tenn. boy, 16, dies by suicide after classmates out him by sharing sexually explicit texts." *Yahoo News*. October 1, 2019. Retrieved from https://www.yahoo.com/entertainment/tenn-boy-16-dies-suicide-153530028.html.

18. Ibid.

19. Alex Horvath. "Frontier high teacher resigned in exchange for back pay in settlement agreement with KHSD." *The Bakersfield, Californian*. May 10, 2019. Retrieved from https://www.bakersfield.com/news/breaking/frontier-high-teacher-resigned-in-exchange-for-back-pay-in/article_12121e86-736a-11e9-90ca-97f8f7b9b555.html.

20. Todd Love, Christian Laier, Matthias Brand, et al. "Neuroscience of internet pornography addiction: a review and update." September 2015. *Behavioral Sciences* (Basel, Switzerland) 5(3): 388–433. Retrieved from https://www.ncbi.nlm.nih.gov/pmc/articles/PMC4600144/.

21. Staff. "Porn addiction." *PsychGuides: American Addiction Centers Resource*. 2019. Retrieved from https://www.psychguides.com/behavioral-disorders/porn-addiction/.

22. Ibid.

23. Ibid.

24. United States Department of Justice (NSOPW). *The Dru Sjodin national sex offender website*. June 10, 2012. Retrieved from www.nsopw.gov. Cf. State of California Department of Justice, *Megan's law home*. Retrieved from www.meganslaw.ca.gov/.

25. United States Department of Justice (NSOPW). *The Dru Sjodin national sex offender website*.

26. "Sexual predator law." *The Free Dictionary*. Retrieved from http://legal-dictionary.thefreedictionary.com/Sexual-Predator+Law.

27. Staff. "Any youngster with a mobile phone or web access is at risk of exploitation." *This Is Derbyshire*. July 14, 2012. Retrieved from www.thisisderbyshire.co.uk/youngster-mobile-phone-web-access-risk/story-16539284-detail/story.html.

28. Staff. "Trump signs law curbing sex-trafficking websites." *Center on Media Crime and Justice.* April 12, 2018. Retrieved from https://thecrimereport.org/2018/04/12/trump-signs-law-curbing-sex-trafficking-websites/.

29. Staff. "Internet pornography by the numbers; a significant threat to society." *Webroot Cybersecurity Resources.* 2019. Retrieved from https://www.webroot.com/us/en/resources/tips-articles/internet-pornography-by-the-numbers.

30. Julie Ruvolo. "How much of the internet is actually for porn?" *Forbes Magazine.* September 7, 2011. Retrieved from www.forbes.com/sites/julieruvolo/2011/09/07/how-much-of-the-internet-is-actually-for-porn/.

31. Staff. "Internet pornography by the numbers: A significant threat to society." *Webroot Cybersecurity Resources.* 2019. Retrieved from https://www.webroot.com/us/en/resources/tips-articles/internet-pornography-by-the-numbers.

32. Staff. "Internet crime and abuse statistics." *GuardChild.* June 4, 2011. Retrieved from www.guardchild.com/statistics/.

33. Staff. "Sexting." *ASK: The Alliance for Safe Kids.* June 4, 2011. Retrieved from http://allianceforsafekids.org/resources/tips-for-parents/sexting/.

34. Staff. "Rebellious Teenagers." *AllPsychologyCareers.com.* June 3, 2012. Retrieved from www.allpsychologycareers.com/topics/rebellious-troubled-teenagers.html.

35. Gatecrasher. "Sex and the city author Candace Bushnell rejects 'cougar' tag." *New York Daily News.* August 24, 2009. Retrieved from http://articles.nydailynews.com/2009-08-24/gossip/17931305_1_cougar-candace-bushnell-younger.

36. Amy Oliver. "Sex education: why *are* so many female teachers having affairs with their teenage students . . . and is the 'cougar effect' to blame?" *Mail Online.* May 28, 2011. Retrieved from www.dailymail.co.uk/news/article-1391626/Whats-wrong-female-teachers-America-As-schools-summer-young-teacher-arrested-sex-16-year-old-student-latest-dozens-cases-school-year.html.

37. Luke O'Niel. "Incest is the fastest growing trend in porn. Wait, what?" *Esquire.* February 28, 2018. Retrieved from https://www.esquire.com/lifestyle/sex/a18194469/incest-porn-trend/.

38. Serena Gordon. "New study finds some boys are having sex before age 13." *CBS News.* April 8, 2019. Retrieved from https://www.cbsnews.com/news/new-sex-study-finds-small-percentage-boys-having-sex-before-age-13-jama-pediatrics/.

39. Staff. "The list: Celebrities accused of sexual misconduct." *The Morning Call.* September 25, 2018. Retrieved from https://www.mcall.com/entertainment/mc-harvey-weinstein-impact-list-of-men-accused-of-sexual-misconduct-20171129-story.html.

40. Sam Dorman. "James Patterson: Epstein case worse than Weinstein, Cosby allegation, others during #MeToo era." *Fox News.* July 9, 2019. Retrieved from https://www.foxnews.com/us/james-patterson-epstein-worse-weinsteins-cosby.

41. Staff. "20 child actors who have spoken out on abuse." *TV Over Mind.* 2018. Retrieved from https://www.tvovermind.com/20-child-actors-spoken-abuse/.

42. Judith Spitzer. "A hidden crime: Child sex trafficking is on the rise." *The Spokesman Review.* February 13, 2018. Retrieved from https://www.spokesman.com/stories/2018/feb/13/a-hidden-crime-child-sex-trafficking-is-on-the-ris/.

43. Mary Kinney. "Kathy Ireland opens up about sexual abuse in modeling." *AOL*. June 5, 2014. Retrieved from https://www.aol.com/article/2014/06/05/kathy-ireland-opens-up-about-sexual-abuse-in-modeling/20907269/.

44. Kayla Jimenez. "Grooming is a gateway to sexual abuse, but schools are virtually powerless to stop it." *Voice of San Diego*. June 4, 2019. Retrieved from https://www.voiceofsandiego.org/topics/education/grooming-is-a-gateway-to-sexual-abuse-but-schools-are-virtually-powerless-to-stop-it/?fbclid=IwAR1sLVWPmkz5dMXT1Q-hK0WOIc0qbTIqzyPEWS6I2XQMuGpfQr3LUIuSM68.

45. Sharon Jayson. "More college 'hookups,' but more virgins, too." *USA Today*. March 20, 2011. Retrieved from www.usatoday.com/news/health/wellness/dating/story/2011/03/More-hookups-on-campuses-but-more-virgins-too/45556388/1.

46. Jenni Fink. "Is sex addiction a real disorder? Majority if Americans believe it is." *Newsweek*. July 23, 2018. Retrieved from https://www.newsweek.com/sex-addiction-real-disorder-majority-americans-believe-it-1037560.

47. Lina Kim, Claire Rhee, Kyle Wang, et al. "Bellarmine broads' blog: Boys rated female teachers' looks, attractiveness online." *FalconOnline*. February 13, 2018. Retrieved from https://www.saratogafalcon.org/content/bellarmine-broads-blog-boys-rated-female-teachers%E2%80%99-looks-attractiveness-online.

48. Mashable Deals. "Swiping sucks, so here are the best dating sites for men to find love." *Mashable*. July 22, 2019. Retrieved from https://mashable.com/roundup/best-dating-sites-for-men/.

49. Staff. "Inside suspected pedophile's lair, a glimpse at a global child rape epidemic." *New York Post*. May 9, 2017. Retrieved from https://nypost.com/2017/05/09/suspected-pedophile-busted-in-sickening-philippines-sex-den/. Cf. Tom Davis. "Shocking list of defendants in massive NJ child porn bust." *New Jersey Patch*. December 1, 2017. Retrieved from https://patch.com/new-jersey/wall/79-child-predators-busted-massive-nj-porn-operation.

50. Kerry Justich. "Teachers are turning to 'sugar daddy' dating site to supplement their salary." *Yahoo News*. October 1, 2019. Retrieved from https://www.yahoo.com/lifestyle/teachers-on-sugar-daddy-dating-site-to-supplement-salary-145919281.html.

51. NAMBLA. *Wikipedia*. Retrieved from https://rationalwiki.org/wiki/North_American_Man/Boy_Love_Association.

52. Kim, Rhee, Wang, et al. "Bellarmine broads' blog: Boys rated female teachers' looks, attractiveness online." *Falcon Online*. February 13, 2018.

53. Vivian Igra and Charles E. Irwin. "Theories on adolescent risk-taking behavior." 1996. *The Handbook of Adolescent Health Risk Behavior*, ed. Ralph J. DiClemente, William B. Hansen, and Lynn E. Ponton. New York: Plenum Press, pp. 35–51.

54. Ecclesiastes 1:7–11 (NASB).

55. Denise Lavoie, "Vast international child-porn network uncovered." *MSNBC*. August 4, 2012. Retrieved from www.msnbc.msn.com/id/48502531/ns/us_news-crime_and_courts/.

56. Barry M. Leiner et al. "Brief history of the internet." *Internet Society*. August 5, 2012. Retrieved from www.internetsociety.org/internet/internet-51/history-internet/brief-history-internet/.

57. Ibid.

58. Michael Fullan. *Change forces*. 1993. New York City: The Falmer Press, p. 10.

59. Tina Sieber. "What a flash mob is and how you can participate." *MakeUseOf.* October 19, 2010. Retrieved from www.makeuseof.com/tag/flash-mob-participate-examples/.

60. Jessica Firger. "Occupy 2.0: Protesters go hi-tech." *Wall Street Journal.* March 17, 2012. Retrieved from http://online.wsj.com/article/SB1000142405270230 4459804577285793322092600.html.

61. Carol Huang. "Facebook and Twitter key to Arab spring uprisings: Report." *The National.* June 6, 2011. Retrieved from www.thenational.ae/news/uae-news/facebook-and-twitter-key-to-arab-spring-uprisings-report.

62. *ViolentFlashMobs.com.* June 5, 2012. Retrieved from http://violentflashmobs.com/.

63. Annie Vaughan. "Teenage flash mob robberies on the rise." *Fox News.* June 18, 2011. Retrieved from www.foxnews.com/us/2011/06/18/top-five-most-brazen-flash-mob-robberies/; cf. Ian Urbina. "Mobs are born as word grows by text message." *New York Times.* March 24, 2010. Retrieved from www.nytimes.com/2010/03/25/us/25mobs.html.

64. Staff. "Former Fruitland High assistant track coach charged with rape." *KTVB.com.* August 5, 2019. Retrieved from https://www.ktvb.com/article/news/crime/former-fruitland-high-assistant-track-coach-charged-with-rape/277-3a11ca56-dd16-480a-b697-a98226383ed4.

65. Scott Raynor. *Marion Patch.* "Wisconsin teacher accused of having sex with Marion teen allegedly had toddler present in home." April 28, 2012. Retrieved from https://patch.com/iowa/marion/editor-s-pick-wisconsin-teacher-accused-of-having-sex-8daafc3ecc.

66. Christina Schaefer and Courtney Wheaton. "Former Ohio teacher facing sex charges involving 28 first grade girls." *Bakersfield Now Eye Witness News.* June 18, 2019. Retrieved from https://bakersfieldnow.com/news/nation-world/former-ohio-teacher-facing-sex-charges-involving-28-first-grade-girls-06-18-2019.

67. Steve Helling. "Teacher, 51, accused of sexually abusing 14-year-old boy for months: 'It's horrible. I can go to jail.'" *Yahoo News.* September 27, 2019. Retrieved from https://www.yahoo.com/entertainment/teacher-51-accused-sexually-abusing-191958154.html.

68. Staff. "Christine A. McCallum, teacher, accused of having sex with teen 300 times." *Huffington Post.* January 10, 2009. Retrieved from www.huffingtonpost.com/2009/01/10/christine-a-mccallum-teac_n_156867.html.

69. Sarah Beckman. "Des Moines teacher accused of offering sex to teenage student." *We Are Iowa.* May 31, 2019. Retrieved from https://www.weareiowa.com/news/local-news/des-moines-teacher-accused-of-offering-sex-to-teenage-student/?fbclid=IwAR2-_AjzJ5fvGybkJ7yY0PIgYahwLGlBGvpcDoGXazZbh0wX9qEkocx8d0.

70. Staff. "Notorious teacher sex scandals." *CBS News.* 2019. Retrieved from https://www.cbsnews.com/pictures/notorious-teacher-sex-scandals/.

71. Staff. "Female New York teacher accused of having sex with student in motel." *Fox News.* December 1, 2015. Retrieved from https://www.foxnews.com/us/female-new-york-teacher-accused-of-having-sex-with-student-in-motel.

72. Staff. "Report: Biology teacher allegedly raped boy multiple times over summer break." *Digital Media Links*. August 24, 2019. Retrieved from https://dml-newsapp.com/report-biology-teacher-allegedly-raped-boy-multiple-times-summer-break/?fbclid=IwAR0YPo4qcYeZRioOQxA_QvxpefrU95_Xlyy5XBOBitThYTU rwx7v1QEWeSc.

73. Chris Harris. "Married Pa. teachers sexually abused teen girl—wife wanted him to 'get it out of his system.'" *Yahoo News*. June 21, 2019. Retrieved from https://www.yahoo.com/entertainment/married-pa-teachers-sexually-abused-154814750.html.

74. Anthony Alvarez. "Former Arvada High School assistant principal, arrested for alleged sexual relationship with 15-year-old student." *Huffington Post*. September 6, 2011. Retrieved from www.huffingtonpost.com/2011/09/06/anthony-alvarez-former-ar_n_950907.html.

75. Kayla Jimenez. "Teacher accused of molesting elementary student was allowed to quietly retire." *Voice of San Diego*. July 11, 2019. Retrieved from https://www.voiceofsandiego.org/topics/education/teacher-accused-of-molesting-elementary-student-was-allowed-to-quietly-retire/?fbclid=IwAR2yfb1dSZYZ0XiY4_4Jb TfY941_hOlJoybOMPSi8ARAmdU4MoJkpvI-mvI.

76. Crosby Shaterian. "Miramonte head soccer coach accused of sex with minor." *KERO 23 Bakersfield News*. February 28, 2012. Retrieved from www.turnto23.com/news/30554301/detail.html.

77. Laura Hibbard. "Kacy Christine Wilson, former teacher, allegedly had sex with 16-year-old student in school closet." *Huffington Post*. May 8, 2012. Retrieved from www.huffingtonpost.com/2012/05/07/kacy-christine-wilson-former-teacher-pulls-student-sex-in-closet_n_1496839.html.

78. Staff. "Former Fresno middle school teacher sentenced to a year in jail for sex crimes with student." *Yahoo News*. June 13, 2019. Retrieved from https://www.yahoo.com/news/former-fresno-middle-school-teacher-014228262.html.

79. Molly Crane Newman. "Bronx teacher who performed oral sex on 14-year-old gets 10 years' probation, avoids jail, keeps teaching certificate." *New York Daily News*. September 13, 2018. Retrieved from https://www.nydailynews.com/new-york/bronx/ny-dori-myers-bronx-teacher-sentenced-probation-20180912-story.html?fbclid=IwAR20-Zbkh-13wTg6V2zgHVVktwjXq9LsiovG489QRg-Q1L9QQ7rvy3Z0P0M.

80. Staff. "Assistant cheerleading coach arrested for allegedly performing sexual acts on student." *Fox News*. November 28, 2015. Retrieved from www.foxnews.com/us/2012/06/21/assistant-cheerleading-coach-arrested-for-allegedly-performing-sexual-acts-on/.

81. David Blanchette. "New Berlin schools, former teacher sued over 1980s sex abuse allegations." *The State Journal Register*. September 11, 2018. Retrieved from https://www.sj-r.com/news/20180910/new-berlin-schools-former-teacher-sued-over-1980s-sex-abuse-allegations?fbclid=IwAR1jAhxFHAcwcHIhK1BHDEz9xrV TWt_JLvMYcEJgO5b87XY9qFY_wZzLR9c.

82. Staff. "Former band teacher gets three years for sex crime." *The Bakersfield Californian*. June 28, 2012. Retrieved from https://www.bakersfield.com/archives/

former-band-teacher-gets-three-years-for-sex-crime/article_e14c603c-4c9d-5930-abfd-a71affa2a1ef.html.

83. Jason Bartolone. "Freedom High teacher, Notre Dame standout charged with sex with minor." *Tampa Patch*. August 19, 2011. Retrieved from http://newtampa.patch.com/articles/teacher-ex-football-standout-charged-with-sex-with-minor.

84. Staff. "Disturbing details of Jordan Baptist school teacher alleged sex assault of students released in court, bond set at 750K." *Yahoo News*. July 3, 2019. Retrieved from https://www.yahoo.com/news/disturbing-details-jordan-baptist-school-225144800.html.

85. Chris Harris. "Louisiana elementary school teacher allegedly raped her 10-year-old student." *Yahoo News*. May 3, 2019. Retrieved from https://www.yahoo.com/entertainment/louisiana-elementary-school-teacher-allegedly-181011644.html.

86. Rhonda Eisenberg. "Teacher who gave birth to student's child will be fired school district says." *Huffington Post*. August 3, 2012. Retrieved from www.huffingtonpost.com/2012/08/03/rhonda-eisenberg-teacher-_n_1738724.html.

87. Jeff Truesdell. "Ex-school nurse admits to sex with teen after trying to bribe him with $2,000 car payment." *Yahoo News*. August 12, 2019. Retrieved from https://www.yahoo.com/entertainment/ex-school-nurse-admits-sex-181924585.html.

88. Kathleen Miles. "Anthony Serrano, boxing coach, arrested on suspicion of molesting teen boxer." *Huffington Post*. July 17, 2012. Retrieved from www.huffingtonpost.com/2012/07/17/anthony-serrano-boxing-coach-arrested-photos_n_1680523.html.

89. Ruby Gonzalez. "Ex-Rowland elementary teacher gets 5 years for inappropriately touching 5 students." *San Gabriel Valley Tribune*. March 21, 2019. Retrieved from https://www.sgvtribune.com/2019/03/21/ex-rowland-elementary-teacher-gets-5-years-for-inappropriately-touching-5-students/?fbclid=IwAR37VxVPavdpt2-fptDAddyyl153i5orzpz8Gou9YfXxNGkvSSpoFslk7Rc.

90. Robert Gearty. "Ex-Arizona teacher sentenced to 20 years in prison for sex with student." *Fox News*. July 12, 2019. Retrieved from https://www.foxnews.com/us/ex-arizona-teacher-sentenced-to-20-years-in-prison-for-sex-with-student?fbclid=IwAR3oF_lAuBT0U7KpjYCtmtM1cP-XbuvaROpYHnduLw_ok5YmHQ5xgqoWjQw.

91. Mark Barber. "Woman accused of raping teen with ex-husband, in court next month." *Fox54 News*. June 25, 2012. Retrieved from www.wfxg.com/story/18818088/woman-accused-of-raping-teen-with-former-husband-in-court-next-month.

92. Joe Price. "Texas substitute teacher fired after filing porn in classroom." *Yahoo News*. June 26, 2019. Retrieved from https://www.yahoo.com/entertainment/texas-substitute-teacher-fired-filming-191657718.html.

93. Ian Smay. "Hayden elementary school teacher arrested for sex abuse of a minor charges." *KTVB.com*. April 1, 2019. Retrieved from https://www.ktvb.com/article/news/crime/hayden-elementary-school-teacher-arrested-for-sex-abuse-of-a-minor-charges/293-889abbc0-70db-4efc-8084-45b3b2abf38b.

94. Staff. "Middle school vice principal gets 3 years for sex act with teen girl." *The Bakersfield Californian*. August 7, 2019. Retrieved from https://www.bakersfield.com/news/middle-school-vice-principal-gets-years-for-sex-act-with/

article_c9a006f4-b973-11e9-9d17-e7be890ffc15.html?fbclid=IwAR3UgtsJqG2nfrA mzwJNPlzpwKjaL-3z_st1C6_7Rr0nsHq42_BEp8zWBjk.

95. Staff. "Teen molested by catholic school teacher gets record $8-million settlement from LA. Archdiocese." *KTLA.com*. April 16, 2019. Retrieved from https://ktla.com/2019/04/16/teen-molested-by-catholic-school-teacher-gets-record-8-million-settlement-from-la-archdiocese/.

Chapter 3

America's Sex Culture Affects Teachers and Students

Stacy Halas shocked Southern California and rocked her male students when it was discovered last month that she had a porn-star past. You never saw boys pay attention like they did the day they spotted her work. But, strangely she's not the only instructor. . . . Perhaps parents should be concerned, because there's a healthy history of educators who have worked in the industry.[1]

When the term *American sex culture* is used, there is no doubt that various images are formed in the minds of most people. But taking it to such a level of specificity and understanding its intersectional involvement in our nation's schools can be quite distressing. Drilling down even deeper and associating a culture of sex with American education itself—specifically with implications of improprieties between teachers and students—should be beyond alarming.

Teacher-student sex is the taboo once relegated only to steamy fiction, with its tawdry and salacious book covers. Sex has always been an issue in American culture. Music groups of many eras have sung about sex and sometimes the sex involved relationships with teachers. Hollywood movies have periodically celebrated the teenagers who were able to score with their teachers. Exposing children to sexual content by involving them in movies that contain gratuitous sex was once off-limits. Now, children are placed in adult-like roles with the expectation the audience will see them that way.

Sex between teachers and students has been a part of the American literary, entertainment, and fantasy world for a very long time. A simple search online will yield just how many authors and musicians spend their moments reflecting on their experiences and their fantasies. The difference today is that such ideas, desires, and experiences are more out in the open. The advent of the Internet, social media, and immediate recording and posting through smart devices has changed the landscape of the sex culture. Rather than in the background below the surface, sex culture now appears completely mainstream.

AMERICA'S SEX CULTURE

American culture can be defined by sex. It is part of America's new identity. On the scandal side, headlines are replete with sexual miscues between pastors and parishioners, athletes and coaches or trainers, musicians and fans, actresses and actors, politicians and constituents, and yes, teachers and students—ranging from elementary schools to colleges.

Teachers and students fill just one segment of sex-saturated American culture. But it is not just school teachers who are experimenting with sex, both in real terms and online. The Internet is a keyword search away from people who have filmed their own pornographic movies and earning money for their activities. Public and private school teachers are also involved in the industry[2] and have made poor character decisions and harmful choices and gotten involved with their students in sexual relationships.

Among the many reasons for the occasions of teachers to make poor choices is the hours spent in close proximity with their students. In fact, some "students spend more than 1,000 hours with their teacher in a typical school year," depending on the grade level. Even with this number of hours spent together, this used to be the actual academic scope of their relationship. Now, the hours spent often exceed the 1,000-hour mark through all kinds of avenues, both at school and from home. Relationships develop over time, and the more time spent together, the greater the likelihood that something could go wrong and the relationship could "go totally off the rails."[3]

Therefore, what is meant by the term *American sex culture* may conjure different connotations for the readers. In terms of this chapter, *the denotation of sex culture pertains to the prevalence of sexual content and sexual practice that are both mainstream and accessible with ease through various portals, regardless of one's age, sex, or gender*. The Internet is one such major portal.

Other portals include cable and satellite programming, as well as smart technology applications, public school literature, sex and romance genres, video games and sex-figure animation, modeling profession,[4] Hollywood entertainment, online dating, adult escort massage, and sex sites. Through all the fog that emanates from such a list, there are some teachers directly in the midst of the mist. They are shooting homemade and staged sex acts and are finding such practice a lucrative monetization through their own personal adult websites.[5] This is also part of a growing trend within America's sex culture where teachers falsely believe their private lives only affect their off-hours exploits.

Panoply of Sex

In focusing on sex culture, many sexual orientations are on display. The LGBTQ+ communities have made sex a front burner issue in society. Their powerful and well-resourced lobbies not only support their causes but also stand behind the movement. Each year there are parades celebrating and flaunting sex practices during PRIDE celebrations. It is not uncommon to see nakedness and sexual activity at these parades. Even scantily clad children appear in the parades and on side streets performing for adults. The author has witnessed such an activity.

But parades and public displays are not the overall intention for the LGBTQ+ lobby. The goal is to affect the minds and hearts with sex and gender so as to capture the attention and fragile emotions of students. This is being accomplished under the guise of tolerance and inclusion, but disallowing dissent.[6] To this end, the LGBTQ+ communities have gained access to bureaucrats and politicians, intending to radically change the education policy and public schools across the nation. America's sex culture is also highly politicized. One might ask, how do groups bring sexuality into schools?

Groups like GLSEN, PFLAG, and GLAAD bring sexuality into schools through conducting assemblies, literature, online communications with students, assisting in the formation of Ally Clubs, Gay-Straight Alliances, contributing to state-level school curriculum decisions, helping to organize protests, and serving as monetary and resource activists on behalf of sex and gender issues in schools.[7] It is politically incorrect to stand against these organizations, even if the stance is morally correct on behalf of children.

LGBTQ+ groups are spearheading efforts to make certain that children are able to read about and understand history, social science, and sexuality from diverse viewpoints. By diverse, they mean from a viewpoint that steers far from the traditional curriculum. California and New Jersey[8] are leading the way with legislation mandating LGBTQ+ inclusions into public school curriculum. In many ways, the LGBTQ+ culture has become a driving force toward sexualizing American children.

Sexual Content

Parents have spoken out about sexual content in literature for as long as it has been published. They continue to speak out, but their voices are being drowned out by groups no longer willing to tolerate dissent. Parents are expressing concerns about the transition of alternative sexual behavior in literature to the enculturation of all things sex and gender in public schools. America is not alone in their concern. In 2019, several employees resigned their posts at England's National Health Service because children were being[9] "misdiagnosed as transgender and given harmful and irreversible hormone treatments."

Back in 2009, in the state of Kentucky, some parents were upset at some of the literature selected by high-school teachers for students to read. One parent directed communication to the Montgomery County School Board about the literature used in co-ed high-school classes, claiming, Risha Mullins, the teacher at the time, "taught soft pornography."[10]

Incidents like these were not uncommon in recent history. Limits have always been tested, whether from a traditional or progressive perspective. But they have accelerated with the explosion and saturation of sexual content in the mainstream. The alleged *soft porn* sex culture of 2009 pales in comparison to what took shape just a decade later. In fact, the mainstream media is questioning whether there is any such thing as "good porn."[11] Here is a case in point. Ironically, the principal who banned the books in question in the Kentucky case in 2009 was recently arrested and "charged with 30 counts of child pornography-related offenses."[12]

Latina Ana Samuel writes about what she discovered in her children's school district-approved Language Arts curriculum: "What is heteronormativity and how is it harmful?"[13] Sex is now found in curriculum in all subjects in grades K–12. "It is not unusual for the LGBT theme to find its way into history classes, foreign language studies, and even STEM courses. The explicit goal is to normalize LGBT lifestyles throughout curricula."[14] Additional concerns found by CanaVox, the parent group founded and directed by Samuel, include the following:

> Pediatricians who ask to see our daughters alone and then push to prescribe them contraceptives or ask about sexual behaviors that we find offensive. Our teens themselves bring these pediatricians' inappropriate behavior to our attention. . . . Sex education class in which our kids are taught unproven Freudian-Kinseyan doctrines that sexual repression will cause neuroses . . . and which preach about topics like abortion, masturbation, condom use, sex toys, outercourse, oral stimulation, and rectal intercourse . . . while refusing to seriously address the short and long-term medical and psychological risks of these actions . . . [p]ublic library programming where unicorns, rainbows, gingerbread persons, drag-queen story hours, and other symbols of progressive sexual ideology make an appearance . . . [t]rendy middle-school books (published after 2014) that appear to have fairly innocuous plots frequently feature an LGBT teen or gay couple, ever-so-gently normalizing the ideas that are conflicting to our consciences . . . [a]nd last but not least, the latest round of violence against children: efforts to entice children to question the reality of their sex through school gender-transitioning ceremonies, pronoun sensitivity training, and other transgender propaganda. . . . Now activists are pushing courts to allow minors to receive puberty-blocking drugs and cross-sex hormones against their parents'

objections. . . . Mothers are very good at educating and protecting our children from harm when we believe they are in danger. This time, that danger is the sexual ideology of the far left.[15]

Planned Parenthood is either present on many school campuses or accessible in providing sex counseling. They also have been known to assist young girls and teenagers before and after their pregnancies. Schools that allow Planned Parenthood to teach sex education classes sometimes do not inform parents about the group's presence on campus. A lack of information to parents and the ability for parents to opt their children out have caused controversies at schools.

One such controversy occurred at California's Pacific Grove Middle School, where parents were not told of Planned Parenthood's presence on campus. As an example of what was taught by the group to middle schoolers, California's new sex education law "requires schools to teach the emotional aspects of sex, the possibility that people may have more than one sexual partner, same-sex relationships, and different genders."[16]

Parents were quite upset because they assumed California's sex education would be about traditional biological explanations of sex and disease prevention. But this was not the case. "Your genitals don't make you a boy or girl,"[17] according the Planned Parenthood. As one parent stated, "Now it seems like something that's pushing kids a certain direction, pushing certain viewpoints, especially with the fusion of gender ideology, gender expression, and gender identity."[18] Add this to the fact that California's teenagers "need permission to leave campus, they do not need approval for birth control, abortions, or prenatal care."[19]

In Baltimore, Maryland, in another action outside of parental view, a girl was recently injured because a school nurse was found to have improperly inserted contraception into her body. This was done without parental knowledge or consent.[20] Consent has taken on new focus in public education, given the success and attention afforded by the #MeToo movement. The movement originally arose from allegations and arrests of sexual harassment and sexual abuse of high-profile figures.[21] Nevertheless, when it comes to children in public schools, consent is diminished or sometimes completely disregarded. Why do schools sometimes feel empowered to expose children to elements of culture, the likes of which many parents disapprove?

Like all movements that are used beyond their original purposes, there are spin-offs. For example, "middle school students in Oregon are speaking out about their school district's 'discriminatory' dress code policy." The students argue that the policy "induces rape culture."[22]

In what is becoming the empathetic norm among Generation Z students, one teenager describes "how being called out for dress code violations can make students feel ashamed, hurt, small, not relevant, ugly, and Un loved and embarrassed."[23]

Another teenage student at the school believes that the dress code induces rape culture because "it tells guys if she is wearing short shorts, then she is asking for it."[24] The consensus among girls among the Salem, Oregon, Middle School was that the dress code upset both girls and boys because public shaming of the girls can have an effect on the boys.[25]

Sexual Consent

The Guttmacher Institute found that there are currently only "10 states and the District of Columbia [that] require that consent be part of sex ed curriculum."[26] Although there are different concepts surrounding consent, and varied definitions of the term, the states that require some instruction on consent include California, Connecticut, Maryland, New Jersey, Illinois, Oregon, Rhode Island, South Carolina, Vermont, and Virginia.[27] The argument for pressing for consent instruction is that vagueness leads to sexual abuse and possible violent sexual crimes.

For example, Rhode Island is "one of the few states where it is perfectly legal for teachers and other school employees to have sexual relations with their students once they turn 16."[28] However, some states include clauses "about people in authority"[29] which, in some cases, changes the age of consent to 18. Given that the scientific reality is that students' brains are not yet wired up, they are incapable of weighing the moral choices that come along with life-altering decisions. Consequences have not yet found residency in the emotions and souls of most students. What looks like consent to a teacher might be the result of a manipulated emotions, immature feelings, and *groomed and assumed* permission granted by a student. Permission is not necessarily legal consent, even for mature adults.

But America's sex culture presses onward, giving little thought to consequences and maturity, always seeking to enable people to experience things at younger and younger ages. How does one hold culture accountable? Culture is about beliefs and practices of people and groups. One holds culture accountable one circumstance at a time, one day at a time. Allowing change to occur without resistance is a compromise already in action.

When it comes to sex and public schools, there is no mistaking the fact that America's sex culture is affecting students earlier and earlier, empowering students to avoid informing their parents of their sexual activity. As an example of what schools think about students and their sexual activities, condom distribution is also prevalent on school grounds in America. This coupled with the fact that "local school districts play a big role in shaping sex education curriculum"[30] leave schools open to being accused of drafting policy that is contradictory and "intentionally vague."[31] Vagueness can lead to distorted conclusions.

Sex as Work

To make matters more concerning, legalized prostitution is gaining acceptance in the mindsets of Americans. But America is not alone. South African physician and reproductive specialist Tlaleng Mofokeng thinks "it is not right or just for people who exchange sexual services for money are criminalized and I am not for what I do."[32] In Mofokeng's peculiar justification, he insists that "the idea of purchasing intimacy and paying for the services can be affirming for many people who need human connection, friendship, and emotional support. Some people may have fantasies and kink preferences that they are able to fulfill with the services of a sex worker."[33]

So, girls will begin to figure out that their young bodies have a cash value, and, just like with drug trafficking, they will begin to argue about how they can make more money in one day than their friends can in a week. Also like drug trafficking, sex trafficking is illegal,[34] and it is also a killer.[35]

Mofokeng views more attention to sex work as a plus. The International Labor Organization estimates that "sex workers support between five and eight other people with their earnings. Sex workers also contribute to the economy."[36] They also help to compromise morality and spread a throng of serious diseases of which middle and high schoolers are not necessarily being made aware.[37]

Conversely, in the words of Carol Roth, "if you ask any parent what they want their kid to do for work when they grow up, you would be hard-pressed to find one who would say 'a prostitute.'"[38] In twenty-first-century America the fact that such a *choice* would even be a legitimate *career option* demonstrates how far into the sex culture our nation has delved and descended.[39]

How long before states remove the red-letter stain of current illegal sexual activity by law, (1) include the sex workers as minorities with identities and protected status, (2) offer college courses, and (3) begin to train and educate those seeking majors eventually to work in the adult sex or pornography industry or both? Ultimately, the motivation for the progressives is the movement toward removal of negative stigma of anything associated with the sex industry.[40] This all shakes out to being able to include all aspects of sexuality in children's curriculum and literature and embed sex throughout all content areas.

This is not far-fetched in the least. Consider the facts and the trends. It was only more recently that the LGBTQ+ movement became an acceptable part of public education. Pedophilia and pederasty are quickly becoming acceptable conversations in schools as both the attraction and practice of sex with boys are moving toward being protected and accepted as sexual orientations.[41] Students are learning about alternate lifestyles in their sex education curriculum. Gender has been redefined. What were once taboo sexual practices are now mainstream.

Pornography Goes Mainstream

Pornography is accessed as a sensual daily diet for many Americans, including the fastest growing interest group in females. Lawmakers are scrambling to contend with pornography and what health organizations are calling a "public health crisis."[42] There is only one place to go with a culture already saturated with sex. The last area that has some modicum of protection is children. With states finagling their ages of consent and decriminalizing some of the sexual offenses committed, the next wave of the America's sex culture is approaching the shore. That which was underground is now above ground and there are millions of potential, willing customers and participants. Unfortunately some of these currently occupy American school classrooms as teachers and students.

One major difference in the sex culture of today's America is that an interested sex customer does not have to go to a store discretely in order to view graphic pornographic images. The sex culture is now much more brazen. People, including teachers, now record their sexual activities and post them on a number of worldwide porn sites.

For instance, one former teacher turned to having sex with a seventeen-year-old, after a fight with her boyfriend. After being fired from her teaching position, she then went on to strip and subsequently ventured into filming porn in order to pay her bills.[43] In lieu of jail time, the former teacher was placed on probation, after claiming she was the victim in the months-long relationship, where she had sex with her student hundreds of times.[44]

As evidence of efforts to be considered as mainstream, owners of a well-known porn site based in Miami, called *Bang Brothers* (BangBros), which is a porn reference, recently made a financial pitch to the rights to rename the professional NBA athletic arena the BBC (BangBros Center) in Miami, Florida.[45] BangBros is the same porn group that purchased a website, PornWikiLeaks, "a site that doxed thousands of porn performers."[46] The site outed the names of performers, "but it often added other personal information such as addresses, social media platforms, and the names of family members."[47] More than 15,000 porn performers were outed by the site. Sex has become so mainstream due to the Internet that its purveyors now see fit to protect the identities of popular adult sex performers and discard those who are outed.

Women and girls are a growing audience for pornography. Female and male teachers are filming their sex acts and posting them online,[48] thinking nothing will happen to their careers.[49] After all, they think they are filming on their own time.[50] Porn addiction for men, boys, women, and girls is a growing problem. Relationships are skewed because of the objectivizing of females as sex objects. Men, in efforts to make extra cash, contract out their bodies for gay sex films, even though they may not be gay. The financial short-term gains attract all-too-willing participants.

Teenagers are questioning their sexuality and experimenting. They are told that their gender and sexual expression are fluid. Teachers are being fired for not using proper sex or gender pronouns that students prefer in class. The fact that sex and gender blurring is now incorporated into schools is another indication that America's sex culture has as much to do with confusion as it does with political correctness.

HOW BAD IS THE PROBLEM?

Another aspect of today's sex culture is the rampant spread of sexually transmitted diseases, usually by having sex with multiple partners. States have been reexamining their ages of consent to adjust them upward.[51] But they talk a great game when it comes to combatting what most Americans see as problems with predators, registered sex offenders, and pedophiles. To no one's surprise, sexual abuse is an ongoing major problem in America.

A study commissioned by the American Association of University Women in 2000 concluded that an estimated 10 percent of students suffer some form of sexual abuse during their school years.[52] The study centered on eleventh graders, who filled out surveys full of personal questions. In addition to lewd comments, exposure to pornography, and being groped and viewed in locker rooms, the researchers also discovered the students had been victimized by specific groups of people, including teachers, coaches, administrators, and various school employees.

More recent data has been compiled by the Children's Center for Psychiatry, Psychology and Related Services and the organization Stop Educator Sexual Abuse Misconduct and Exploitation (SESAME).[53] The numbers indicate that "children in 8th through 11th grade, about 3.5 million students (nearly 7 percent surveyed reported having had physical sexual contact from an adult (most often a teacher or coach). The type of physical contact ranged from unwanted touching of their body, all the way up to sexual intercourse. This statistic increases to about 4.5 million children (10 percent) when it takes other types of sexual misconduct into consideration, such as being shown pornography or being subjected to sexually explicit language or exhibitionism."[54] The problems have increased dramatically over the course of a decade, due in large measure to the advancements in technology and the political pressure to accept alternate sex and gender philosophies and practices into the mainstream.

The perception of negative consequences has been diminished and risk-taking has been enhanced with the advent of smart technology. There is a pseudo-sense of privacy people seem to enjoy because of technological advancements. This sense of privacy really is a mere perception and not a reality.

Hardly anyone these days is without a smartphone in America. In fact, "the vast majority of Americans—96 percent—now own a cellphone of some kind."[55] What people do with their phones has changed over the years. Smartphones are now primary devices for businesses, academic research, and social media contacts. They are also used as recording devices, watching videos, playing video games, listening to music, as well as for voice and text communications. Access to the world is literally in people's hands each day. As a result, people are in touch with more choices, various options, including seductive temptations that expose children to immoral practices.

Regrettably, "the Department of Justice notes that about 15 percent of children in the 12–17 age group who own a cell phone have received nude, semi-nude, or sexually suggestive images of someone they know via text. 11 percent of teenagers and young adults say they have shared naked pictures of themselves online or via text message. Of those, 26 percent are trusting enough to think the person to whom they sent the nude pictures wouldn't share them with anyone else. About 26 percent of teenagers and young adults say they have participated in sexting."[56]

Trust is becoming less valued by smartphone users and it is easy to lock out others from seeing what is done with it. Personal privacy means a lot to people while on the Internet and with interpersonal communications. But teenagers are not private when it comes to those things that elevate their status among peers.

As a former Beaumont High School discovered, teenagers communicate about their activities in ways that elevate their personal status. Among the many victims of sexual abuse by the teacher, one wrote: "Yes . . . bro, I', gettin' in deep . . . been f****** [her] and getting threesomes for the past couple of weeks at her house."[57] In a strange twist, the teacher, Samantha Ciotta, did not have to register as a sex offender, and it is possible for her to reapply for another California teaching license in the near future. The nation may be on the verge of complete dismantling of residual morality. How long before teachers who sense strong temptations to have sex with their students are actually allowed to do so by law?

THE ALLUREMENT

One of the reasons teachers allow themselves to become so emotionally connected with some of their students is the basic immaturity of the teacher. Youthful, vibrant teachers who share interests with students, spend time teasing about their favorite sports teams, have lunches together to listen to shared music interests, or just seem to hit it off sometimes have more in common than they do with their own families.

Despite the age differences the joy that emerges from spending time together leads to more time together. This reinforces the emotional connections. Soon, the teacher finds it acceptable to continue the feelings from home, and the relationship is established beyond acceptable boundaries.

Emotional connections are quite alluring and, in a culture of sex, the dangers are taking these feelings to deeper levels by physical and sexual contacts. The fact that a teacher would think about, fantasize about—or even joke about—anything physical indicates that the teacher has fallen into a trap. Thus, the teacher has been seduced by his or her own emotions and convinced that what is felt is real and genuine. It's as if they are in an adult dating relationship.[58] Marianne Garvey asserts that "many don't understand boundaries and honestly don't fully grasp that they are actually committing a crime, either."[59]

A second reason teachers cross into the danger zone with students is a popular teacher seeks to extend this sense of popularity. This is another way of vicariously realizing what they missed while they were students in school. Being popular with boys or girls and projecting back to their past, unfulfilled longings is another example of a void in an immature teacher. Similarly, a teacher who is not fulfilled at home, is on the rebound from a relationship gone badly, or is lonely is inclined to reach out to students for attention.[60]

A third reason for teachers being lured into relationships with their students is the fact that they are pedophile predators. Teachers may not have come to terms with their own abuse when they were children. But as adults, they have become the hunters as well as the hunted.

Being a victim results in no background check and the external signs are usually absent at the time of hire. Teachers in these situations must be honest about their past and seek help. But the risk of losing something for which they worked so hard overrides the consideration of any personal admission on the front end of employment opportunities. Skilled interviewers must find ways to determine risk factors resident in teacher candidates.

Another reason for teachers crossing boundaries with students is the human sex drive. The social media posting site Reddit[61] abounds with teachers discussing colleagues who either have had sex with students, are currently having sex with students, or wish they could.[62] Both male and female teachers discuss everything from lust for sexual pleasure as a cause, revenge for another person's breakup with them, to regret for their actions. Some even post suggestions about ways to keep sex with students a secret.

One additional reason is the positional differential between teachers and students. In this age of sexual saturation, dominant and submissive sexual practices became mainstream with *Fifty Shades of Grey*, and its sequels. Sex toys and tools, dungeons, restraints, whips, and a number of alternative lifestyle implements are now common knowledge to so many students. Sex is a tool for power, even if manifested through role-playing and arcane practices.

Sex and Power

Teachers have the authority in a classroom and students are under this authority. Often some students will challenge this authority and savvy, mature students and will seek to chip away at the authority of a teacher and take this task to heart. Teachers willing to give away some of their authority play directly into the reality that students are empowered to be the center of the education universe. It is a perfect storm for dominant and submissive role-play.

For example, as the submissive, whether teacher or students, the person yields to the power display of the dominant. There is willingness to allow this exchange. In the minds of those involved, emotional satisfaction may be derived by one, while the exchange of power is providing physical pleasure to the other. This form of relationship is based on *trust* and *safe words*. Teachers who see their students' *adult-like maturity* and carnal knowledge as fruit to be tasted have a skewed sense of sexuality. If teachers are as tempted to have sex with children as they are as tempted to have sex with adults, they may fall into the submissive category emotionally and want to be taken as such. This being taken is a way to please the dominance they perceive within the student's personality.

On the flip side, there may be teachers seeking to be the first sexual partner for students. This dominance can be as predatory as other expressions of sex, but the fulfillment is realized in both the arousal of the student and the teacher's conquest of taking a student's virginity. These comprise the ultimate expressions of power. Predators manipulate emotions through this power to secure the confidence of children with the ultimate goal of sexual contact. Most teachers are probably not predators, in that sense.

Whether students are sexually dominant or submissive should have no place in the minds of teachers. Teachers who dabble or delve into the Dom-Sub or BDSM lifestyles have no business teaching children. Students are not yet wired up. Teachers might have short circuits due to past abuse. Sex is an emotional experience that requires two mature adults, and those adults are best married. Generally, the emotions associated with the practices of casual sex can be both devastating in the present and lead to sexual abuse in the future.

AMERICAN HYPERSEXUALITY

America's sex culture is partly responsible for the nation's hypersexuality. That which is in our faces regularly can either numb the senses or compel with relentless mental force, or both. However, sex between consenting adults is one thing. Believing that sex with children and minors is acceptable means there are other factors at work beyond sex. The fact that more young female teachers seem to be falling into the trap of sex with their students, and in some cases multiple students involving hundreds of times, means that there must be more than sexual fulfillment and sexual conquest involved.

One reason for the increase of hypersexual performances may be connected to biology and emotions. Chair of the psychiatry department at Mt. Sinai Hospital in New York, Eric Hollander, writes that "when women become hypersexual, the number one disorder that seems to drive that hyper sexuality in women is bipolar disorder."[63] Hypersexuality of some teachers and the hyperemotional states of average teenagers make for a potentially dangerous combination—especially when attractions seem natural and feel good to the parties involved.

Hollander's conclusions open the door for school districts to ask whether future employers should know about a prospective teacher candidate's bipolarity, which could very well become a major issue when working with students. Why take the risk? The risk is taken because districts are forbidden to ask about such personal issues. Yet teachers are allowed to post their "sexy" photos on social media pages and film their own pornography, in some cases, and keep their jobs?

Gaining Affection

Gaining the trust of teenagers and their parents and then encouraging teenagers to make important decisions based on emotions are two tactics used to win the affections of potential victims. Once there is an emotional connection between a would-be-predator and a victim, the connection only strengthens with private communications. Therefore, when emotional bonds are deeply forged, it is only a matter of time before the temptation of physical attraction sets in. The following two examples illustrate these points.

Example 1: Coach

Coach M is a physical education teacher with tenure. He is also the varsity girls' soccer coach at a local high school. He is thirty-three years old and single and enjoys his work. He is thought to be personable and fun. Some of the players on Coach M's team live in rural areas. So, after practice—and after some evening games—the coach routinely transports a small number of female players to their homes.

During the course of a season, Coach M is accused by some players of playing favorites and paying special attention to one player in particular. Girls complain off the field and on their social media pages. Rumors abound among the players, eventually escalating among students on campus. One of the allegations made is that the teacher/coach is having an affair with one of his players. The administration checks into the rumors and downplays them. Parents are notified and they begin to pay extra close attention.

All seems settled, until after one game, when Coach M is transporting one of his sixteen-year-old players to her home. While in transit, and driving a district van, the coach stops at a liquor store to purchase some items. One of these items was condoms. The female clerk notices the teenage female sitting in the van's passenger seat, the district logo on the van, and the age differential between the man and the teenager. This raises her suspicions. She calls authorities, and the school district is contacted the next day. Coach M is arrested, eventually put on trial on a variety of sexual molestation charges, including sexting a minor, and is found guilty.

Example 2: Mrs. J

"Mrs. J" is a newer addition to the high school where she once sat as a student. Her smile and personality are engaging. Her accomplishments as an athlete are storied, and her reputation as a coach at the school and in the community is now beginning to take hold. One high-school sophomore girl begins spending extra time with Coach J after practices. The well-meaning coach drives her home on occasion.

Over the course of a season, the two chat online some evenings, texting and photo messaging increases, and a different sort of relationship forms between the female player and female teacher-coach. One evening, the player and coach begin kissing and fondling each other in the coach's car while parked in a dimly lit area of the school parking lot. They are caught. The coach is dismissed from her teaching and coaching job and subsequently arrested, tried, and convicted of sexual assault.

Cultivating Emotional Connections

The nature of most students is not to remain in close contact with their teachers, while on breaks. Few middle- and high-school students seek to remain in contact with their teachers while away from school, and for good reason. In attempts to ensure this remains the case, states are implementing policies that strongly recommend that teachers not contact students at home for social purposes. Adults socializing with children are evidence of extensions of emotional bonds that are formed in classrooms. These bonds are red flags.

Students often seek access to school information from home but not necessarily the teacher who comes along with the information. Athletics and academic events often require home communication, but these communications should involve the parents in the loop. All things considered, as a rule, academics should be the primary focus for any communication with students or players.[64] Even with states' best efforts, some teachers seem intent to cross into inappropriate relationships with students.

In April 2012, twenty-five-year-old Pennsylvania teacher Timothy Moll was accused of sending text messages to one of his students, a sixteen-year-old female student, offering her decent grades in exchange for her indecent photographs.[65] In March of that same year, substitute teacher Michael Zack allegedly sent four teenage female students over 4,000 text messages with several inappropriate photographs attached to some of the texts. He and the students were also found to be communicating during school hours via Facebook and text messaging.[66] Losing sight of the academic purposes of education and forming emotional bonds with one or more students only lead to other issues.

Generally, teacher-student contact at home should not be permitted. As often as possible, teachers or coaches who are talking with students or athletes while at home need to inform parents of the conversations and contexts, which makes this regular contact less risky. It is a good rule to involve parents in as much of the communication with their teenagers as possible.

A good general rule to follow is that home contact should not be viewed as strictly social. Home contact should always be treated as formal. The closer a teacher comes to a sociable, *friend-like* relationship with his or her students at school or at home, the greater the risk of something—a word, photograph, or action—being misconstrued. All it takes is one mistake or one allegation to ruin lives and careers.

Table 3.1 lists six principles for teachers to consider when communicating with students after-hours.

Table 3.1   Six Principles for Appropriate After-Hours Communication between Teachers and Students

Principle 1: Brevity Is Best
• Keep message exchanges with students brief and to the point.

Principle 2: Flirts Are Potential Hurts
• Avoid any flirtatious communication.

Principle 3: Shun "Forward" Thinking
• Never forward any personal photographs or post anyone else's photographs to a student's cell phones or social networking pages.

Principle 4: Permissions Have Conditions
• Do not upload anything to do with a current student's social media page to any teacher or parent social media site without parental consent. If the data or photos in question are of a school function or activity, the teacher should get parental consent in writing.
• Often, high schools have forms for students and parents to sign granting permission for students to both access the Internet and appear online in photograph, if they represent the school in athletics or activities.
• Be professional in deciding what to post online.

Principle 5: Seeing Is Believing
• Err on the side of "more information to parents is best." Always CC—or carbon copy—the text message or e-mail communication you have with the student to the student's parents, unless the parent waives this action.
• If a parent will not allow access to his or her cell phone number through texting, then it is probably best not to allow his or her teenager to mine.
• This same forwarding rule applies to e-mail as well. If parents do not have e-mail, a computer, or a cell phone but the teenager does have access to these, it is incumbent upon the teacher to lay out the ground rules to inform the parent.
• Teachers can serve parents in many ways: one is to provide some education about the technology their teenagers are using most every day.

Principle 6: Arm's Length Means a Leg Up
• Beware of the number of messages sent to students and teachers.
• Remember, the closer one gets to another human being, the greater the chances of relating on personal levels.
• Teachers should beware how close they get to their students emotionally.
• Do periodic proximity checks: If you notice students drawing closer to you than you would like, parents should be informed. Some students do stalk their teachers for attention. Share these signs of closeness with administrators and student's counselors.
• Minute usage and numbers contacted are records that are easily discovered. Check the minutes used and text messages you send to particular numbers.
• Make certain there is a balance so as to avoid any notion of impropriety. Doing so might very well open the lines of communication and head off any possibility of a problem at the point of origin.

In another incident, Erica DePalo—the 2011 Essex County, New Jersey, Teacher of the Year—was accused of having a sexual relationship with one of her fifteen-year-old students. She allegedly began the affair with her West Orange High School English honors student on June 15, 2012, and ended the affair on August 28, 2012, the week prior to the beginning of a new academic school year.

DePalo was arrested and charged with several sex crimes with a minor. Technology obviously played a role in keeping the emotional bond alive throughout the summer of 2012.[67] What purpose, other than desires of intimacy, would a teacher have during summer to stay in close contact and get together in private sexual dalliances with her teenage male student?

Teachers seeking affection from children as if they were adults implies there is something broken within the teachers. Their actions, emotional connections, and sex with the children only perpetuate the brokenness in their lives and plant the seeds of potential sex abuse to affect another generation. Teachers must have the following dictate drilled into their heads: *A student is never a teacher's soulmate.*

EFFECTS OF AMERICA'S SEX CULTURE UPON TEACHER-STUDENT RELATIONSHIPS

America's sex culture has affected teacher-student relationships in many ways. The effects of today's sex culture have become quite obvious. Smart technology and what is viewed on devices has shifted the ways teachers and students come to view each other.

For example, the billions of pornographic images and videos online provide an ample supply of selected inputs to occupy a person's attention for a lifetime. A simple Google search of the term *sex culture* returned over 740 million results. A mental diet of sex will program a student's mind and imagination to view his or her teacher as an object of desire as well as a challenge to be met. This is much more than a crush on a personality.

One student admitted to the author that he watched porn occasionally in his sophomore English teacher's class so he could lust after her while she taught. He also admitted that he and a few friends shared the videos with each other during group work. Another student related that his science teacher had her own porn site, so he watched her personal sex videos during her class and became physically aroused and ultimately distracted by her presence.

Smart technology has been a game changer in the development of teacher-student relationships. America's sex culture has also impacted teacher-student relationships by a saturating sexuality, so that children and adults become preoccupied with it. When children grow up "in a highly eroticized sexual environment—a legacy of the sexual revolution—American children are preoccupied with sex in developmentally distorted ways and increasingly likely to act out their sexual impulses."[68]

Teachers who are immature may very well be affected by the same preoccupation and find themselves acting on similar impulses. Psychologist

Tom Lickona writes: "The widespread sexual harassment in schools and the rising rates of teen sexual activity are not isolated phenomena but an outgrowth of the abnormal preoccupation with sex that children are manifesting from the earliest grades. . . . The sexual corruption of children reflects an adult sexual culture in which the evidence continues to mount that sex is out of control."[69] Lickona wrote these words in 1993 and the children at the time who went to college to become teachers are now in front of America's children.

America's sex culture has impacted teacher-student relationships because of the focus on one's sexual and gender identities. Students confused about their biology and emotions find it difficult to comprehend a world of black and white through their lens of gray. Students who feel that their job is to be an active advocate for sexuality place pressures on teachers. Teachers are left to determine how best to navigate the student-centered classroom, while being pressured by their districts and square student pressure with the academic expectations of their states.

When teachers become objects for students and this practice is not corrected, students cross into territory that makes it easier to make comments and flirt with teachers. America's sex culture, in many ways, has made women and girls into objects. On the one hand, highly charged sexuality brings on expressions of this sexuality. On the other hand, political correctness and the law mandate that people practice self-control and restraint. People are divided by these today. When teachers are treated as such, respect is greatly diminished and the normal, professional teacher-student relationship is headed in the wrong direction.

When coupled with choices and temptations and a much more open sex culture, those involved find it easier to cross over into emotional, physical, and sexual realms. When any one of these crossovers occurs, the results can lead to ruined personal relationships, losses of employment, arrests, conviction, prison, registration as a sex offender, loss of teaching licenses, corruption of minors' morals, and rejection by families and friends. The sex culture in prison is vastly different.

Students as victims can be scarred for life. As a result of becoming involved with teachers, sometimes students choose to harm themselves. They also turn to drugs or find other adults who may victimize them. There is a guilt and remorse that generally follows once the novelty wears off. They can also become abusers of children later in life.

In contemporary America, the lines of respect for human sexuality are no longer in place. Students know this and teachers know this. Boundaries must be reestablished and clearly delineated in terms of what is, and what is not, acceptable for relationships between teachers and students.

SUMMARY

American culture can be defined by sex and teachers and students fill just one segment of America's contemporary sex-saturated society. Among the many reasons for the occasions of teachers to make poor choices is the hours spent in close proximity to their students. Relationships develop over time. The more time that teachers and students spend together increases the risk of something going wrong.

The term *American sex culture* may conjure different connotations for the readers. In terms of this chapter, *the denotation of sex culture pertains to the prevalence of sexual content and sexual practice that are both mainstream and accessible with ease through various portals, regardless of one's age, sex, or gender.* The Internet is one such major portal.

In focusing on sex culture, many sexual orientations are on display. For example, the LGBTQ+ communities have made sex a front burner issue in society. Their powerful and well-resourced lobbies not only support their causes but also stand behind the movement. LGBTQ+ groups are spearheading efforts to make certain that children are able to read about and understand history, social science, and sexuality from diverse viewpoints. By diverse, they mean from a viewpoint that steers far from the traditional curriculum. The explicit goal is to normalize LGBTQ+ lifestyles throughout curricula, thereby normalizing what used to be categorized as alternative lifestyles.

Planned Parenthood is either present on many school campuses or accessible in providing sex counseling. They also have been known to assist young girls and teenagers before and after pregnancies. Schools that allow Planned Parenthood to teach sex education classes sometimes forget to inform parents about the group's presence on campus. A lack of information to parents and the ability for parents to opt their children out have caused controversies at schools.

The Guttmacher Institute found that there are currently only 10 states and the District of Columbia [that] require that consent be part of sex education curriculum. What looks like consent to a teacher might be the result of a manipulated, immature, and groomed permission granted by a student. Permission is not necessarily legal consent, even for mature adults.

One major difference in the sex culture of today's America is that an interested sex customer does not have to go to a store discretely, in order to view graphic pornographic images. The sex culture is now much more brazen. Women and girls are a growing audience for pornography.

Female and male teachers are filming their sex acts and posting them online, thinking nothing will happen to their careers. After all, they think they are filming on their own time. Porn addiction for men, boys, women, and girls is a growing problem. Also, relationships are skewed because of the objectivizing of females as sex objects.

Teenagers are questioning their sexuality and experimenting. They are told that their gender and sexual expression are fluid. More recent data has been compiled by the *Children's Center for Psychiatry, Psychology & Related Services* and the organization SESAME. The numbers indicate that children in 8th through 11th grade, about 3.5 million students (nearly 7 percent) surveyed reported having had physical sexual contact from an adult and increases to about 4.5 million children (10 percent) when it takes other types of sexual misconduct into consideration.

One of the reasons teachers allow themselves to become so emotionally connected with some of their students is the basic immaturity of the teacher. Emotional connections are quite alluring and, in a culture of sex, the dangers are taking these feelings to deeper levels by physical and sexual contacts.

A second reason teachers cross into the danger zone with students is a popular teacher seeks to extend this sense of popularity. Three additional reasons include: (1) teacher predator-pedophilia, (2) the human sex drive, and (3) the positional differential of power between teachers and students.

The Department of Justice notes that about 15 percent of children in the 12–17 age group who own a cell phone have received nude, semi-nude, or sexually suggestive images of someone they know via text.

Generally, teacher-student contact at home should not be permitted. A good general rule to follow is that home contact should not be viewed as strictly social. Home contact should always be treated as formal. The closer a teacher comes to a sociable, *friend-like* relationship with his or her students at school or at home, the greater the risk of something—a word, photograph, or action—being misconstrued.

America's sex culture has impacted teacher-student relationships because of the focus on one's sexual and gender identities. Students as victims can be scarred for life. Boundaries must be established to reexamine and clearly define what is, and what is not, acceptable in terms of relationships between teachers and students.

DISCUSSION QUESTIONS

1. Define the term *sex culture*.
2. What characteristics are present in a culture of sex?
3. In what ways has America's sex culture ensnared teachers and students?
4. What reasons can you provide as to why teachers would consider having emotional, physical, or sexual relationships with students? Why is this thinking wrong?

5. How has the LGBTQ+ movement opened doors to sexuality in American public schools?
6. How does pornography affect the ways students might perceive teachers?
7. What are your views on the statement *what teachers do on their own time is their own business*?
8. What are some good general rules to maintain proper teacher-student relationships, both at school and at home?

NOTES

1. Dennis Romero. "Porn-star teachers are nothing new: Our all-time top 5." *LA Weekly*. April 3, 2012. Retrieved from https://www.laweekly.com/porn-star-teachers-are-nothing-new-our-all-time-top-5-photos/.

2. Staff. "Porn actress claims Christian school fired her from teaching job because of her sex films." *Fox News*. June 26, 2017. Retrieved from https://www.foxnews.com/us/porn-actress-claims-christian-school-fired-her-from-teaching-job-because-of-her-sex-films.

3. Sarah D. Sparks. "Why teacher-student relationships matter." *EdWeek*. March 12, 2019. Retrieved from https://www.edweek.org/ew/articles/2019/03/13/why-teacher-student-relationships-matter.html.

4. Georeen Tanner and Angela Bertorelli. "'Predators like Jeffrey Epstein familiar faces in seedy 'underbelly' of the modeling world." *Fox News*. September 28, 2019. Retrieved from https://www.foxnews.com/entertainment/jeffrey-epstein-predator-models.

5. Hannah Parry. "Ohio band teacher quits after school is tipped off to her secret life as an internet porn star." *Daily Mail*. September 17, 2015. Retrieved from https://www.dailymail.co.uk/news/article-3238643/Ohio-band-teacher-quits-school-tipped-secret-life-internet-porn-star.html.

6. Martin M. Barillas. "Iowa boy and family fear retribution for resisting LGBT propaganda at school." *Lifesite News*. October 4, 2019. Retrieved from https://www.lifesitenews.com/news/iowa-boy-and-family-fear-retribution-for-resisting-lgbt-propaganda-at-school.

7. Samuel Smith. "NJ law forcing schools to teach LGBT history is about 'indoctrinating' students, critics say." *Christian Post*. February 12, 2019. Retrieved from https://www.christianpost.com/news/nj-law-forcing-schools-to-teach-lgbt-history-is-about-indoctrinating-students-critics-say.html. Cf. Steve Strunsky. "Mayor says LGBTQ+ curriculum will 'indoctrinate' kids and his successor agrees." *NJ.com*. October 9, 2019. Retrieved from https://www.nj.com/ocean/2019/10/mayor-says-lgbtq-curriculum-will-indoctrinate-kids-and-his-successor-agrees.html. Cf. Hannan Adely. "How will LGBT history be taught in New Jersey schools after new law?" *North Jersey Record*. February 7, 2019. Retrieved from https://www.northjersey.com/story/news/education/2019/02/07/

nj-law-requires-schools-to-teach-lgbt-history-but-implementation-unclear/27790010
02/?fbclid=IwAR0VK1dKLymBqK4lX_uF-Ei7YzosGLkMmVMugAq0khSmbOHe
6Sy6_4MnQcw.

8. Smith, "NJ law forcing schools to teach LGBT history is about 'indoctrinating'
students, critics say."

9. Mairead McArdle. "Employees quit NHS transgender clinic over kids'
experimental treatments." *National Review*. April 8, 2019. Retrieved from https://
www.nationalreview.com/news/employees-quit-nhs-transgender-clinic-over-kids-
experimental-treatments/.

10. Billy Kobin. "Kentucky principal who faces child porn charges once
banned books with 'homosexual content.'" *Louisville Courier Journal*. August 29,
2019. Retrieved from https://www.courier-journal.com/story/news/local/2019/08/29/
kentucky-principal-facing-child-porn-charges-once-banned-books/2149974001/.

11. Ian Kerner. "Is there such a thing as 'good porn'?" *CNN*. March 13, 2018.
Retrieved from https://www.cnn.com/2016/11/07/health/ethical-porn-ian-kerner/
index.html.

12. Kobin, "Kentucky principal who faces child porn charges once banned books
with 'homosexual content.'"

13. Ana Samuel. "A message to Mayor Pete from a Latina mama: 'Don't force
your sexual ideology on me and my children.' *The Public Discourse*. April 17, 2019.
Retrieved from https://www.thepublicdiscourse.com/author/ana-samuel/.

14. Ibid.

15. Ibid.

16. Robin Abcarian. "A school decided to let Planned Parenthood teach sex-
education classes. Trouble ensued." *Los Angeles Times*. April 12, 2019. Retrieved from
https://www.latimes.com/local/abcarian/la-me-abcarian-sex-ed-20190412-story.html.

17. Ryan Bomberger. "Planned Parenthood, LGBT Inc and comprehensive sex
miseducation." *Christian Post*. March 28, 2019. Retrieved from https://www.christian
post.com/voice/planned-parenthood-lgbt-sex-miseducation.html.

18. Abcarian, "A school decided to let Planned Parenthood teach sex-education
classes."

19. Ibid.

20. Doug Mainwaring. "Mom solves daughter's mystery illness: School nurse
secretly inserted birth control implant." *LifeSite News*. October 3, 2019. Retrieved
from   https://www.lifesitenews.com/news/teens-mystery-illness-solved-school-
nurse-inserted-iud-without-parental-consent?utm_content=buffer853e4&utm_
medium=LSN%2Bbuffer&utm_source=facebook&utm_campaign=LSN&fbclid=Iw
AR0cV7i1xG1ZKKk3yPZd4S1jBDhf-T-uw13kkfgj3A2EHlm.

21. Ronan Farrow. *Catch and kill: Lies, spies, and a conspiracy to protect predators*.
2019. New York: Little, Brown, and Company. Cf. Brian Flood. "6 takeaways from
Ronan Farrow's bombshell interview for 'catch and kill.'" *Fox News*. October 10, 2019.
Retrieved from https://www.foxnews.com/media/ronan-farrow-catch-and-kill.

22. Mahira Dayal. "Students slam school dress code: 'It tells guys if she is wearing
short shorts she's asking for it.'" *Yahoo News*. June 18, 2019. Retrieved from https://
www.yahoo.com/lifestyle/students-slam-school-dress-code-205050915.html.

23. Ibid.

24. Ibid.

25. Ibid.

26. MaryClaire Dale. "Amid #MeToo, states debate teaching consent to kids." *The Associated Press.* May 19, 2019. Retrieved from https://www.apnews.com/bc44860de19948df89e645f325a6add9.

27. Ibid.

28. Erika Sanzi. "Both teachers' unions oppose bill that would make sex with students a crime." *Good School Hunting.* April 3, 2019. Retrieved from https://good-schoolhunting.org/2019/04/teachers-unions-oppose-bill-make-sex-students-crime.html?subscribe=success#blog_subscription-3.

29. Ibid.

30. Dale, "Amid #MeToo, states debate teaching consent to kids."

31. Ibid.

32. Tlaleng Mofokeng. "Why sex work is real work." *Teen Vogue Magazine.* April 26, 2019. Retrieved from https://www.teenvogue.com/story/why-sex-work-is-real-work.

33. Ibid.

34. Adeel Hassan and Katie Van Syckle. "Porn producers are charged with sex trafficking." *The New York Times.* October 13, 2018. https://www.nytimes.com/2019/10/11/us/porn-sex-trafficking.html.

35. Alex Lasker. "Sex trafficking victim, 15, commits suicide after return to family: 'We got her back damaged.'" *AOL.* October 17, 2019. Retrieved from https://www.aol.com/article/news/2019/10/17/sex-trafficking-victim-15-commits-suicide-after-return-to-family/23840417/.

36. Mofokeng, "Why sex work is real work."

37. Staff. "Risk, ethics & sexually transmitted diseases: High school bioethics." *New York University School of Medicine.* 2019. Retrieved from https://med.nyu.edu/highschoolbioethics/briefs/risk-ethics-std.

38. Carol Roth. "Carol Roth: No teen vogue, you should not promote prostitution as a career choice." *Fox News.* June 22, 2019. Retrieved from https://www.foxnews.com/opinion/carol-roth-no-doctor-you-should-not-promote-prostitution-as-a-career-choice-to-teens.

39. Ibid.

40. Ibid.

41. Alex Newman. "Pedophilia being taught as 'sexual orientation' in California schools." *Freedom Project.* April 17, 2019. Retrieved from https://www.winterwatch.net/2019/04/pedophilia-being-taught-as-sexual-orientation-in-california-schools/. Cf. Olivia Messer. "Teacher at elite boarding school used nightly 'check in' system to molest sleeping students, cops say." *Yahoo News.* October 9, 2019. Retrieved from https://news.yahoo.com/teacher-elite-boarding-school-used-175215377.html.

42. Louis Casiano. "Porn a public health crisis in US, Arizona and other states agree." *Fox News.* May 12, 2019. Retrieved from https://www.foxnews.com/health/arizona-follows-lead-of-other-states-in-calling-pornography-a-public-health-crisis.

43. Staff. "Iowa teacher busted for sex with student turns to porn." *Mandatory.* March 23, 2017. Retrieved from https://www.mandatory.com/living/1236121-iowa-teacher-busted-sex-student-turns-porn.

44. Peter Holley. "'I feel like I was the victim': Former high school teacher blames student for seducing her." *Chron.* October 21, 2016. Retrieved from https://www.chron.com/news/article/I-feel-like-I-was-the-victim-Former-high-10042884.php.

45. Dillon Thompson. "BangBros Center: Porn site bids $10 million to rename Miami Heat's NBA arena." *AOL.* September 13, 2019. Retrieved from https://www.aol.com/article/finance/2019/09/13/bangbros-center-porn-site-heats-nba-arena-american-airlines-stadium-basketball/23812401/.

46. Brenden Gallagher. "Bang Bros, bought a website that doxed porn performers—and burned all its files." *The Daily Dot.* August 30, 2019. Retrieved from https://www.dailydot.com/upstream/bang-bros-porn-wiki-leaks-fire/.

47. Ibid.

48. Staff. "13 teachers who were also porn stars." *eBaum's World.* May 9, 2015. Retrieved from https://www.ebaumsworld.com/pictures/13-teachers-who-were-also-porn-stars/84563115/.

49. Slate Video Staff. "Porn-star teacher? Tera Myers loses job over X-rated past." *Slate.* March 9, 2011. Retrieved from https://slate.com/news-and-politics/2011/03/porn-star-teacher-tera-myers-loses-job-over-x-rated-past-video.html.

50. Staff. "Stacie Halas, fired Calif. teacher with porn past, loses appeal." *CBS News.* January 16, 2013. Retrieved from https://www.cbsnews.com/news/stacie-halas-fired-calif-teacher-with-porn-past-loses-appeal/. Cf. Dennis Romero. "Porn-star teachers are nothing new: Our all-time top 5."

51. Staff. "Ages of consent & sexual abuse laws around the world." *AgeofConsent.net.* 2019. Retrieved from https://www.ageofconsent.net/.

52. Brian Palmer. "How many kids are sexually abused by their teachers? Probably millions." *Slate.com.* February 8, 2012. Retrieved from www.slate.com/articles/news_and_politics/explainer/2012/02/is_sexual_abuse_in_schools_very_common_.html.

53. Jason Kotowski. "Open talks recommended between parents and children regarding allegations of educator abuse and inappropriate behavior." *The Bakersfield Californian.* February 2, 2019. Retrieved from https://www.bakersfield.com/news/open-talks-recommended-between-parents-and-children-regarding-allegations-of/article_e2161860-263c-11e9-8d1f-efbf2c4be6fd.html.

54. Staff. "Sexual abuse by teachers is on the rise." *The Children's Center for Psychiatry, Psychology, & Related Services.* July 11, 2017. Retrieved from https://childrenstreatmentcenter.com/sexual-abuse-teachers/.

55. Staff. "Mobile fact sheet." *Pew Research Center.* June 12, 2019. Retrieved from https://www.pewinternet.org/fact-sheet/mobile/.

56. Staff. "Sexual abuse by teachers is on the rise." *The Children's Center for Psychiatry, Psychology, & Related Services.* July 11, 2017. Retrieved from https://childrenstreatmentcenter.com/sexual-abuse-teachers/.

57. Renee Schiavone. "Why a CA teacher who had sex with a student is not a 'sex offender.'" *Patch.* May 16, 2018. Retrieved from https://patch.com/california/banning-beaumont/ca-teacher-who-had-sex-student-not-sex-offender.

58. Marianne Garvey. "Why so some teachers risk everything to have sex with their students?" *Bravo.* December 28, 2017. Retrieved from https://www.

bravotv.com/personal-space/why-do-some-teachers-risk-everything-to-have-sex-with-their-students.

59. Ibid.

60. Jamie Poole. "Why do high school teachers (female) sleep with their students in USA?" *Quora*. December 26, 2016. Retrieved from https://www.quora.com/Why-do-high-school-teachers-female-sleep-with-their-students-in-USA.

61. "Teacher sex: Reddits and sub-Reddits." *Reddit*. 2019. Retrieved from https://www.reddit.com/r/TeacherSex/.

62. Garvey, "Why so some teachers risk everything to have sex with their students?"

63. Matt Lauer. "Crossing the line: An interview with Debra Lafave." *Dateline NBC*. September 13, 2006. Retrieved from http://www.nbcnews.com/id/14499056/ns/dateline_nbc/t/crossing-line/#.XaDEqkZKiUk. Cf. Brian Flood. "NBC news labeled an 'unrepentant boys club' amid latest sordid allegations." *Fox News*. October 11, 2019. Retrieved from https://www.foxnews.com/media/nbc-news-boys-club-ronan-farrow.

64. Ernest J. Zarra, III. *Detoxing American schools: From social agency to academic urgency*. 2020. Lanham, MD: Rowman & Littlefield Publishers.

65. Laura Hibbard. "Timothy Moll, former Pennsylvania teacher, accused of exchanging good grades for student's nude photos." *Huffington Post*. April 5, 2012. Retrieved from www.huffingtonpost.com/2012/04/05/timothy-moll-former-teacher-accused-of-exchanging-good-grades-for-nude-photos_n_1407026.html.

66. Nikki Krize. "Substitute teacher accused of inappropriate behavior." *WNEP.com*. March 16, 2012. Retrieved from http://wnep.com/2012/03/16/substitute-teacher-accused-of-inappropriate-behavior-4/.

67. Mike D'Onofrio. "High school female teacher from Montclair arrested for sex with student." *Montclair Patch*. September 3, 2012 Retrieved from http://montclair.patch.com/articles/high-school-female-teacher-from-montclair-arrested-for-sex-with-student. Cf. "Erica DePalo, former 'teacher of the year,' allegedly had sexual relationship with student." *Huffington Post*. September 3, 2012. Retrieved from www.huffingtonpost.com/2012/09/03/erica-depalo-teacher_n_1852369.html.

68. Thomas Lickona. "Where sex education went wrong." *Educational Leadership* (November 1993) 51(3):84–89. Retrieved from http://www.ascd.org/publications/educational-leadership/nov93/vol51/num03/Where-Sex-Education-Went-Wrong.aspx.

69. Ibid.

Chapter 4

Relationships between Teachers and Students

The mother . . . called the teacher and recorded the conversation . . . the teacher allegedly said she had become pregnant with the teen's child and had had an abortion. She also said she was in love with the student. . . . The student was 17 at the time.[1]

How do educators decide how close is too close in terms of relationships with their students? Educators face a real dilemma in trying to find a balance between expectations and reality as they weigh the proper professional distance they ought to keep from students, while seeking to remain relevant and personable.

Students' passions and interests are always shifting. This means certain moral and ethical beliefs that undergird adults' practices are not yet well-demarcated in students. The last thing students need are teachers who either compromise their own morals and ethics or have not yet progressed far enough in their own to understand the meaning of boundaries.

As was stated in chapter 2, the brains of adults are not fully wired up until their mid-to-late twenties. In a culture saturated with sex, willing partners whose brains are not yet developed with consequential thinking could miss the mark in understanding choices and their subsequent actions. Teachers must present clear lines of boundaries. If they are unable to do so, they should not be present in classrooms, or working with students. However, one cannot assume today that when a teacher is hired that these clear boundaries are understood.

HOW CLOSE IS TOO CLOSE?

Examples found in recent headlines are repulsive.[2] Across this nation, some teachers use social media indiscreetly, setting poor examples by posting sex-related comments, sexual photographs, or comments or photographs involving alcohol or drug use. The fact is there is an epidemic of teachers being arrested for having sexual relationships with students and more females than males seem to be garnering the headlines.

A fifty-six-year-old Illinois Language-Arts teacher was found guilty of sexual abuse and assault of a seventeen-year-old female student. Records indicated he and the student exchanged more than 700 text messages. Similarly, a thirty-seven-year-old California high-school band director pleaded guilty to sexual misconduct with a sixteen-year-old female student. Her Facebook page recorded over 1,200 private messages from the band director. In the state of Pennsylvania, a thirty-nine-year-old male high-school athletic director was arrested for offering gifts to a former male student in exchange for sex. He was convicted on the charge of attempted corruption of a minor. Technology played a role as the primary means of fueling the relationships.

Notice a pattern? Teachers are far too close to students when they are regular buddies, dismantling the natural age boundary that exists between them. For the sake of protection of students' well-being and guarding of careers, there must be well-stated and clear guidelines of proximity for teachers and students today.

SUGGESTED GUIDELINES OF PROXIMITY

Teachers are too close to students when their professional proximity blends into an individual, discrete, and personal relationships during school hours and off-hours. This type of proximity is the foundation for serious moral and educational compromises. Generally, students begin to notice changes in the way one or two students are treated once proximity boundaries have been crossed.

For the sake of clarity, proximity concerns become evident when teachers' relationships with students (1) distract from the mission of the school, (2) provide emotional confusion for students and teachers, (3) manifest themselves by undercutting or usurping family time and undermine the values of teachers or students, or (4) assume that teachers and students share a very special connection or emotional bond because of feelings.

Please read those four statements of concern again. If a teacher's relational proximity is compromised by any one of these, he or she needs to reevaluate how close he or she is to his or her students. Any acceleration of student-teacher proximity means an emotional bond may have been created, which has all the earmarks of eventually turning physical.

Shared Activities

Most teachers genuinely care about students from wholesome hearts and work academic and social wonders with their students. This is not a coincidence and the results can be amazing. According to DeRoche and Williams, students learn best when they know teachers care about them and are passionate about their content areas.[3] In today's educational environment, students and teachers are drawing more closely together through joint efforts in academic competitions, performances, and various other functions that take their professional relationships outside the school day.[4]

As most education literature asserts, teachers live in a student-centered world. Education, proclaim the bureaucrats, is first and foremost about students.[5] Parents are increasingly relying on schools to assist in the rearing of their children. Accordingly, schools have stepped up the whole child education approach. "At the core of the 'whole child' concept is the understanding that children grow physically, emotionally, and intellectually; therefore, school should attend to all of these areas of growth."[6] More and more parents are using the schools as places to rely on, as well as places to lay blame when things go awry in their children's lives.

THE INAPPROPRIATE AND THE ILLEGAL

There are many examples of good and bad teacher-student relationships in American schools, both public and private. Fortunately, just having a bad relationship probably will not result in an arrest. However, what will lead to eventual trouble, including arrest, jail time, and loss of mostly everything in life, is a teacher's relationship with a student that moves from inappropriate to illegal.

There are arrests made in this nation almost every week that involve teachers, coaches, and even administrators. The criminal charges range from sexual assault to the rape of a child. The effects on the children who are victimized by teachers are traumas that last a lifetime. The same can be true for students in a classroom of a teacher arrested for such victimization. Their lives are affected well into their futures. This also plays out at college, although a bit differently.

Students are not helped at all when colleges do nothing about sex parties or when professors even encourage "love on campus," as did Yale English professor William Deresiewicz in his piece titled "Love on campus: Why we should understand, and even encourage, a certain sort of erotic intensity between student and professor."[7]

What the professor seems not to have considered is that the eighteen-year-old senior in high school is scarcely different from the eighteen-year-old freshman in college. To make matters worse, some teenagers are having sex with their professors in college and there is little outcry. Where are the states' laws restricting these behaviors between persons of authority and their college students? Happily, states are getting serious about passing laws to address and ensure these restrictions.

Teenagers are adults at eighteen, legally. However, what is legal is certainly not always moral and mature. These eighteen-year-olds, off-limits in high school, experience direct erotic exposure and are encouraged to experiment with their legal status as eighteen-year-olds in college. When is an eighteen-year-old not an eighteen-year-old? The easy answer is *at college.*

High-school students do not need erotic exposure, yet it happens. Take, for example, an incident involving a Florida male private school teacher and one of his female students. The single teacher in his mid-twenties developed an after-hours relationship with one of his female high-school students, who was sixteen years old at the time. They had been texting for months, and an emotionally deep relationship had been established. She said they were in love. Consider whether this kind of relationship would have blossomed from just limited academic time the teacher and student had spent together in class at school.

Technology and communication from home and in private are the primary enhancements of student-teacher relational bonds. Late-night chats, arrangements to meet, and liaisons during evening school events grew out of their continued communications, all aided by the use of smart technology.

After the budding relationship was discovered, the pattern of the relationship was revealed. The teacher and his teenage student shared texts and photos, chatted on the computer late into the evenings, and teased each other right in class via smartphone. The teacher actually sent the teenager random text messages during classes, just to *make her smile.* In the beginning, the rest of the class was oblivious to what was transpiring between the private school educator and his female student. The teacher was eventually released from his position because of *an inappropriate relationship* with a female student.

The smart technology addiction and impulsiveness of today's generation is as concerning as it is interesting. Teachers should tread cautiously into this communications' realm. The teacher must take care to remember students do not view their emotional connections with teachers in the same light their teachers view them. However, there are concerns. These kinds of problems between teachers and students are no longer rarities, as illustrated by Mikaela Gilbert-Lurie:

> With the advent of technology and online communication, teachers have perhaps never had more opportunities to foster relationships with their students outside of the classroom. Thanks to social networking, teachers can now communicate with their students through e-mails, texts, and instant messages. Oftentimes, behind the safety net of the screen, teachers forget their roles as mentors and figures of authority. Instead, they fall into the trap of talking intimately as if they were romantic interests and thus potential sex objects. With just a screen and some changing language, in the privacy of their own homes, teachers might forget they are talking to confused, acne-plagued, shy teenagers from their classrooms. Perhaps they enjoy the distraction, attention, or compliments they are receiving, becoming too easily seduced. Teachers seem to be finding themselves unable to separate their professions from their personal lives, a risk they should be able to afford.[8]

Examining Gilbert-Lurie's words a little more closely compels four pertinent questions about the case mentioned earlier. *First,* what made the communication inappropriate? *Second,* what role did the initial flirtation play between the two? *Third,* why would a teacher text something personal or relational to a student while in any class? *Fourth,* what boundaries were compromised by communicating with each other from their homes, late into the evening, and without parental knowledge? Answers to these questions are offered in the following paragraphs.

What made the communication inappropriate? First, the relationship distracted from the mission of the school. One could argue that the teacher had begun the relationship with the school mission in mind. However, that quickly grew into something beyond an academic mission to something personal. Consequently, relational lines were crossed.

What role did the initial flirtation play between the two? Second, the relationship between the teacher and the student was responsible for an emotional confusion in the lives of fellow teachers and students, including their own. The moral lines separating the adult and teenager were blurred by first allowing an emotional connection, then by exploring this connection romantically. The teacher's actions crossed moral boundaries, while the student was involved in trying to discover and establish her own moral boundaries.

Why would a teacher text something personal or relational to a student while in any class? Third, the relationship between the teacher and student undercut—and even usurped—professional and personal values. To this day, families are still feeling the effects of the actions of the teacher's and student's improper decorum. The teacher and student were developing and nurturing an inappropriate teacher-student relationship.[9] The fact that the teacher and student kept their communications private and were not account-able to either of the families in their communications is a serious breach of the family's values.

What boundaries were compromised by communicating with each other from their homes, late into the evening, and without parental knowledge? Fourth and finally, the teacher and student shared an inappropriate emotional bond—one that ought not to be shared by teachers and their students. At no time should an adult, empowered by licensure and authority, believe that a student is a personal confidante and an aide in meeting adult emotional and personal needs.

The teacher who believes that a romantic relationship with a teenager will somehow fill a void in his or her life has issues that need serious attention. Gilbert-Lurie and others are right on point in their conclusions. Student-teacher personal relationships are never all right![10]

Private schools, please take note. The incident in question nearly tore the school apart, because of side-taking, rumor-mongering, and postings on social media sites. Private schools employ teachers who are just as human as everyone else. In some cases, religious beliefs and practices are merely a cover for a person's predatory inclinations, and spending time off-hours with a potential victim is sometimes justified as ministry.[11]

Figure 4.1 provides examples for teachers to understand when they have crossed into a boundary violation. Teachers must steer clear from anything that could cause students harm, as well as understand the penalties they will face if they choose to violate one or more of these boundaries.

Another example of inappropriate student-teacher relations involves an Alabama middle-school special-education teacher. The teacher was also the sponsor of the Fellowship of Christian Athletes club at the school. She was charged with having sex with at least eight high-school students between the ages of fifteen and nineteen.[12] She was arrested and later convicted of several charges. The community was outraged and wondered how such things could happen at the school.

Parents, please take note of this very important accountability plea: *Check your students' cell phones periodically for messages that might be problem-atic.* If parents provide the technology, parents should monitor what goes on with it. Ramping up the accountability with the technology our students are using might very well save a host of people from legal and emotional devasta-tions. Not stepping in might mean future counseling for victims of abuse and derailed relationships going forward.

Consider another incident that involved an administrator in a private Christian school in North Carolina. The administrator was accused of, and eventually arrested for, having sexual relations with one of his teenage high-school students.

POWER TO
PUNISH,
SHAME, OR
BENEFIT

NONSEXUAL
MISCONDUCT

SEXUAL

ROMANTIC AND
FLIRTATIOUS

TEACHERS'
BOUNDARY
VIOLATIONS

PHYSICAL

TECHNOLOGICAL

SPECIAL
FAVORS,
SUCH AS
LOANING
MONEY

EMOTIONAL OR
PSYCHOLOGICAL

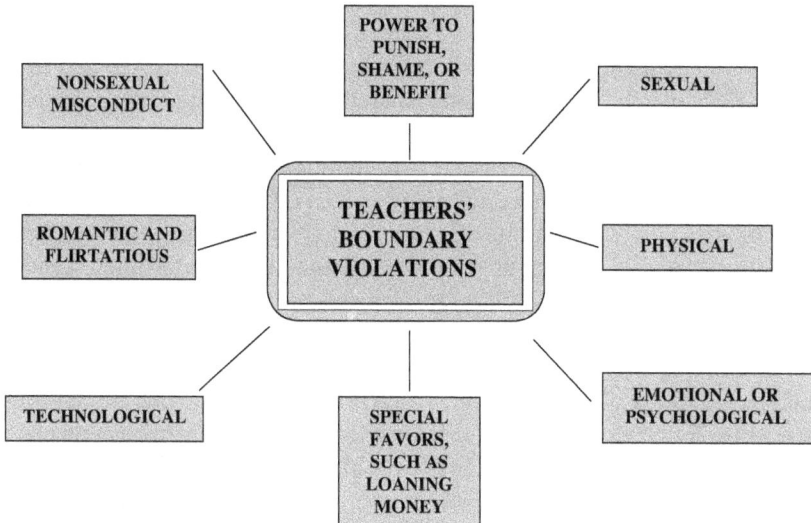

Boundary violations are those where there is harm caused by the violation. Harm generally includes, but is not limited to, the categories of the physical, emotional, sexual, or psychological. Boundary violations also include adverse effects upon a person or persons, or result in negatively impacting the profession, or the community, including reputation loss. Teachers which are greatest at-risk for crossing over into inappropriate teacher-student relationships might include (1) newer teachers, (2) teachers employed in rural or small towns, (3) teachers with close-in-age-proximity, which enables other than a professional relationship to form with students, and (4) teachers whose social, emotional, or mental health is in question.

Figure 4.1   Teacher Boundary Violations
Source: Self-Designed, MS Word

What made this story interesting was that the administrator moved his family to California to escape the legal and community attention. The administrator sought to restart his private school administrative career.

Some months after he was hired in California, he announced he had to return to North Carolina to deal with a case in court that was, in his words, *not really a big issue*. Shortly after, word came down that he was guilty. He was dismissed from his administrative post.

This case was quite personal to me, since I was in the running for the administrative position for which he was later hired. Suffice to say that there are reasons why private schools must always do background and criminal checks of those they intend to hire. Placing too much power in one person to do the hiring is not wise. For further information regarding private schools of faith, on worker screening, refer to my book *It Should Never Happen Here*,[13] for additional safeguards and protective guidelines.

Crossing the Line

Analyses of cases involving teachers and students who have crossed moral boundaries reveal three commonly shared elements. Authors Babchishin, Hanson, and Hermann draw an interesting profile of the "characteristics of online sex offenders,"[14] contending that "online offenders were more likely to be Caucasian and were slightly younger than offline offenders. In terms of psychological variables, online offenders had greater victim empathy, greater sexual deviancy, and lower impression management than offline offenders. Both online and offline offenders reported greater rates of childhood physical and sexual abuse than the general population."[15]

Table 4.1 provides three generalized statements that pertain to teachers and students in sexual relationships. Taken in context, any one of these may be a cause for concern. The three statements yield two conclusions regarding teachers who have sexual relationships with their students. The conclusions are drawn from an analysis of approximately 800 cases and are found following this section in table 4.2.

Shared Trait #1: Past Abuse

In many of the cases examined for this book, two overriding observations are prominent. First, there has been some form of sexual abuse in a teacher's past, and second, the student is absent one or both parental figures in the home. Teachers and students who are in sexual relationships begin these relationships for a variety of reasons.

Psychologists inform us that some students seek attention from teachers in order to fill the void present by the absence of a parent. Some adults naturally step into that role for the sake of the student. Communities applaud teachers, counselors, and coaches who go this extra mile. However, in some cases, it does not end there, and people must ask why.

Table 4.1 Three Shared Traits of Inappropriate Teacher-Student Relationships Leading to Sex

Shared Trait #1: *Past Abuse*	In many cases, there has been sexual abuse in a teacher's past, and the student victim is absent one or both parental figures in the home.
Shared Trait #2: *Unclear Moral Compass*	Teachers and students have allowed emotions to assist them in misreading the moral compasses, resulting in some compromise of moral boundaries.
Shared Trait #3: *Stealth Communications*	Students and teachers engage in ongoing communications and meetings after-hours, without parents being informed.

Friend or Faculty? Jan Wright says:

> When the students are teens, [teachers] walk that fine line between being open enough to get and keep the children's attention and losing their respect as an adult. . . . I have also seen teachers who try to be the students' friend. While this type of teacher might be successful in the short term, teens interact with him/her as they would a friend. Thus, the authority that a teacher must have to structure his knowledge and test the students on how much they know has been lost.[16]

Wright's point is well taken. Teachers who demonstrate personal desires to be students' friends are demonstrating something interpersonal and the actions imply that such friendships can affect more than students' learning. Inappropriate relationships affect all involved and never lead to anything good and wholesome.

Students are intrigued by the novelty and mystery of the unknown. There is no exception when it comes to emotional and sexual possibilities. They may fantasize about the conquest of an older person sexually and then act out their fantasy if the opportunity arises. Others fall prey to manipulation by adults, given substances like alcohol and drugs to soften their wills, and then the exploitation secures them as victims.

Mental Health Issues

Teachers acting out their sexuality with minors have serious mental health issues,[17] normally stemming back to their childhoods. Many of them were likely victims of child sexual abuse, or another forms of abuse, during their formative years.[18] Mullen and Fleming of the American Academy of Experts in Traumatic Stress write that a history of child sexual abuse has been found to be associated with problems with sexual adjustment in adult life. They went on to describe what they termed *reduced sexual esteem* in both men and women who had reported child sexual abuse.[19]

A subsequent study found that women who reported child sexual abuse involving intercourse were significantly less likely to find their adult sexual relationships very satisfactory.[20] As are adults; pressures and circumstances unlock the past, unleashing a fury of consequences affecting the lives of yet another generation. Adults who find emotional solace in children or teenagers, rather than in their peers, are demonstrating that there are unresolved issues that need attention.

Shared Trait #2: Unclear Moral Compass

Teachers and students forming emotional relationships have unclear moral compasses, but for different reasons. Most teenage students are not biologically or emotionally mature enough to have worked out clear moral boundaries. As a result, they rely on their families, their peers, and other authority figures to assist them in the process. Teachers are primary figures and have tremendous responsibility as caretakers. When that trust is violated, it skews moral frameworks going forward.

As addressed earlier in this book, teenagers especially are operating with high levels of dopamine, the pleasure enhancer in the brain. Teachers must acknowledge and affirm that *pleasure* should never be used as a sole gauge to one's decision-making or moral compass—especially among teenagers and their propensity to experiment.

The extreme chemical production in teenagers' brains means their moral decision-making is less a factor in their choices than their impulses driving toward pleasure. This is quite different from when they were younger children. Wynne and Ryan refer to this difference when they assert that "an important part of education consists of posing to students the question, 'What is the right thing to do?' This is a central question in any society, and asking it should begin early and continue through to graduation."[21] Knowledge of this should not be an opportunity for an adult to err and take advantage of a teenager for his or her own adult pleasure.

Any teacher lacking a moral compass must never have access to teenagers. Beliefs about issues or the ability to analyze opposing viewpoints—and even hold to unpopular perspectives about life—are not at issue here. At issue are the behavioral components stemming from these beliefs. Therefore, in every teacher's interviews for hiring, there ought to be several *what if questions* presented to gain an initial gauge of the candidate's beliefs and possible solutions to hypothetical classroom situations.

Errant Moral Compass

A teacher's moral compass can be considered errant if (1) the teacher has no basis to judge whether individual actions are wrong outside of their own beliefs and if (2) the teacher acts for self and does not demonstrate concern as to whether anyone else thinks their beliefs and actions are moral. Unclear moral compasses will eventually lead to serious concerns and these concerns may lead to harmful errants actions. The addition of a culture that has shifting moral boundaries only complicates matters for those still seeking to establish their own. The bottom line is that teenagers need healthy moral mentors to assist them through the murkiness of the teenager years.

One case of a teacher having lost her moral compass is the 2009 case of Christine A. McCallum. McCallum was married at the time she was accused of statutory rape for allegedly having sex 300 times with a teenage boy. The sex began when he was just thirteen years old. According to the boy, they had sex on his kitchen floor, while taking showers together, and in various locations throughout both of their houses.[22] Sadly, McCallum is but one of hundreds-to-thousands of teachers to have lost their way navigating America's sex culture.

The extreme actions of McCallum are clearly illegal, and there is no debate over whether an adult should be having sexual relations with a thirteen-year-old. Consider what first had to take place for the initiation of the relationship, prior to anything physical occurring. What thinking went into the breaking down of moral boundaries in order for an adult to even consider that sex at any one time with a thirteen-year-old was appropriate, let alone hundreds of times?

What type of thinking could ever justify this sort of conclusion? The answer lies in the way the teacher justifies what is right and wrong and when the shift in values occurred. Even if the law points due-north, sometimes teachers' actions extend from an inner distortion that has affected their moral and mental mechanisms for determining right and wrong. The bottom line is that it is just impossible to consider that a teacher could fulfill the mission of the school by having sex with a student.

Fantasies and Obsessions

Teachers who exhibit fantasies of relationships with their students, or entertain thoughts of any kind about having sex with teenagers, have no business in the classroom. Likewise, teachers who express obsessive language about students or demonstrate inappropriate behaviors toward these minors have no business being in the profession. This also pertains to teacher's assistants, coaches, and administrators.

Amber Marshall, a twenty-three-year-old teacher's aide in northwest Indiana, confessed in 2005 to multiple sexual relationships with special-education students at Hebron High School. Investigators claimed that Marshall admitted what she did was wrong and knew it was against the law and implied that she chose to do it anyway. She knew it was wrong and did not care that she was sexually exploiting her charges.[23]

In another case, a Wisconsin teacher exploited a fifteen-year-old girl, by "indulging in sexual talks . . . over SnapChat."[24] The student in question "received pictures and videos from the teacher, one of which was a video of her performing a sex act on herself. The two indulged in two sexual encounters outside of school."[25]

In some cases, moral compasses can be off by a few degrees. Over time, one's actions arrive at destinations unplanned. In other cases, moral compasses point to *self*. In the cases of the teacher's aide, the Wisconsin teacher, and others, the latter appears to be the case. The question is how long had the teachers fantasized and obsessed over the thought and images of having sex with their students?

Shared Trait #3: Stealth Communications

It is inappropriate when teachers and students have ongoing personal communications and get together for private meetings after hours. The computer, video cams, and smartphones are terrific tools when used correctly. When used inappropriately, they can become a weapon against morality with repugnant outcomes as the result. When it comes to the development and support of relationships via technology, the ease with which emotional bonds can be created is astounding.

Curiously, even with emoticons and animations, text does not bring with it the facial expressions, tone of voice, or humor sometimes intended. Yet those relying on technology to nurture relationships quickly find themselves gravitating to FaceTime, Zoom, Skype, or a host of other smart video applications. Online camming is the next best thing to being present in the flesh.

There are definite problems associated with beginning and nurturing relationships based on technology. The digital world is easy to misconstrue, emotionally. Herein lies a problem with stealth or secret communications. The secrecy brings with it an aura of indecency, since the communications are between an adult and a child during after-hours. It would be *virtually*—nearly impossible—to develop closeness between teacher and student without such outside-of-class, regular communication occurrences.

Stealth communications occur for reasons of privacy. They are tantalizing and titillating. Secret video chats appeal to the already-extreme private expectations that accompany children in the natural distancing from their parents' authority. Students who score attention through individual off-hours with their teachers, possibly from bedroom to bedroom, are asking for trouble that their brains have probably not yet been able to process. This is where the teacher should know better, in advance.

Teachers must strive for transparency and exemplify proper use of technology in their relationships with students. Parents must require certain rules to be followed at home with the very technology they provide for their children. Even in a perfect world, the question still remains as to whether teachers should relate online at all with their students.

TWO BASIC FLAWS IN THINKING

Teachers who become involved in sexual relationships with students suffer from two basic flaws. They suffer from the *flaw of moral confusion*, by considering self-pleasure over sensibility and logic of their mission as teachers. These teachers are at the mercy of their own confusion. The *second flaw*, which applies to teachers who cross the line with students, is their fundamental *misunderstanding of emotional risk-taking*. Making choices to take risks with students, driven by emotion and self-pleasure, is not logical for teachers. They were not hired for this and it certainly should not be their mission.

Flaw 1: Exaltation of Self-pleasure

Teachers who cross the line and are eventually discovered share some basic shortcomings. The first flaw deals with personal philosophy involving the *exaltation of self-pleasure*. This is convincing oneself that he or she is entitled to pursue the course taken—even if there is knowledge of wrongdoing at the time. They believe in feelings over reason and legality, and they place pleasure over professionalism.

Wrongdoers rationalize by a variety of mental gymnastics, not the least of which is the feeling of empowerment and feeding of ego-driven sensual desires. Therefore, teachers who decide to have sexual relationships with students (1) *express* self over others, (2) *practice* self-justification of wrong over right, and (3) *demonstrate* a lack of concern, denial, or an inability to assess the true effect of traumas upon self and others. There is an overall inability to sense the detriments, consequences, or harms. This inability yields to thinking that everything will work out in the end.

Cases are emerging in our court system in which some teachers accused of engaging in sexual relationships with their students are now beginning to claim they are victims. Again, there is the fundamental rationale founded on self-focus, as well as a peculiar emotional justification for adult criminal action. This is yet another example of how illogical teachers can be when they fall into the deep end. If school interviewers knew this at the interview stage, the risk of abuse would be minimized by knowledge that could be applied to protect other innocents.

Additionally, there are cases where teachers are claiming to be victims of bipolarity in order to explain their hypersexuality as adults. In February 2010, thirty-three-year-old Stacy Schuler was indicted on sixteen counts of sexual battery and several other counts involving minors. Most of the offenses occurred with several high-school football players from the Ohio school where she was employed, and the offenses dated back to incidents that occurred in her home over a six-month period in 2010. Schuler and her lawyers changed her plea in her case from not guilty to guilty by reason of insanity.[26] Why wasn't her sanity an issue at the job interview or while teaching day in and day out?

Another example is administrator Anthony Alvarez. He engaged in a sexual relationship with a fifteen-year-old female student at Arvada High School in Denver, Colorado. Alvarez's wife overheard her husband using X-rated language to someone on his cell phone. It turned out that Alvarez and the teenager had been posting sexual comments to each other on their Facebook pages.[27] In each of these cases, a common denominator is the thought that the self is protected from harm, because feelings overrode moral sensibility. It is almost as if the person committing the crime is in another person's body. What is it about this technology that leads some to take such self-focused risks?

Flaw 2: Illogical, Emotional Risk-Taking

Why would a person who has worked extremely hard to arrive at life's professional calling and spent thousands of dollars and invested time into state credentialing risk throwing it all away over an emotional or sexual relationship with a teenager? Think about the mindset applied to justify the wrongdoing and then trusting a teenager to remain quiet. This is not logical.

What is in their minds? No one really knows what specifically goes on in a person's mind that would lead him or her to take such chances. Whatever is going on mentally, taking such a risk is illogical to the average adult. What is apparent is the lack of logic that coincides with a teacher's errant thinking and unclear moral compass. The sequence seems to play itself out: A lack of morality results in *risky* corresponding actions that are demonstrated through misplaced emotions.

The reality is that some teachers become involved in manipulative romantic and self-centered relationships, seeking sexual pleasures. These occur when passions come across as incomparable and often seem worth the risk over any context of routine life and stable family. Some adults compartmentalize their behaviors into different moral contexts. In other words, one's private life is different from what is done professionally.

Yet the risk of the loss of almost everything, and everyone in life, seems less impacting than a certain compulsion or desire to gain new sexual experiences. A person has to be quite deeply mired within one's emotions and passions for this illogical reasoning to be applied. One example of this very risk-taking is the story of James Hooker and Jordan Powers.

The forty-one-year-old former California teacher dumped his wife and children and moved in with a former student—with whom he'd begun a relationship while he was still her teacher. Their actions shocked the nation. Hooker insisted he had done nothing wrong, as he waited to start a sexual relationship with Powers until after she had turned eighteen and graduated. But this assertion is problematic, as there are indications that the sexual relationship began earlier than Hooker was willing to admit.

Table 4.2 Conclusions of Teachers Who Have Sexual Relationships with Students

Conclusion 1	Teachers decide to have sexual relationships with students to (1) express self over others, (2) practice self-justification of wrong over right, and (3) demonstrate lack of concern, denial, or an inability to assess the traumas and consequences upon self and others.
Conclusion 2	Teachers have sexual relationships with students because of manipulative romantic and self-centered passion, as well as novel sexual pleasure. The excitement of the risk is worth the gamble of losing everything.

While being interviewed by a local newspaper, Hooker proclaimed that their choice would hurt a lot of people but that they had to follow their hearts over the feelings of others. Has anyone asked what prompts a forty-something family man to drop everything, everyone—even his employment—for a sexual relationship with a teenager? In table 4.2, we identify several conclusions that can be drawn from predators like Hooker who have sexual relationships with their teenage students?

The conclusions reached in the earlier cases demonstrate that these teachers value actions that have their basis in emotions and pleasure-seeking. It is the epitome of celebration of self, mixed with an emotional connection and the opportunity to engage in a high-risk thrilling opportunity. Apparently, the risk is worth it to these teachers, demonstrating again how emotions and pleasure comprise the *logic* that drives decisions. In being true to their emotions, they have lost their sense of service to the community.

Rather than seeking the best interests of the students, the teachers become seekers of their own selfish interests and personal pleasures. This is the ultimate in serving self and exemplifies a form of somatic or narcissistic hedonism. Individuals with "narcissistic personality disorder generally believe that the world revolves around them. This condition is characterized by a lack of ability to empathize with others and a desire to keep the focus on self at all times."[28]

TECHNOLOGICAL ADVANCEMENTS
CHANGE RELATIONSHIPS

Technology has changed the nature of relationships in many ways—and not just between teachers and students but also more broadly between children and adults. The possibility of constant communication with others is quite alluring. According to Robert Sidelinger, "Internet tools allow people to have more freedom and comfort in their interpersonal interactions. CMC (computer-mediated communication) allows people to use hyper personal communication . . . this form of communication occurs when individuals find it easier to express themselves in mediated contexts than in face-to-face situations. CMC offers individuals the freedom to express themselves in positive or negative ways."[29] This may explain why some people have very different online personas and relate differently than they do in person.

With each technological change, the nature of relationships changes, as well. Today there are long-distance relationships between couples and families made easier by video and live-streaming communications. Our military men and women rely on video chats for regular communications with their families. Oil company's ocean-platform workers and engineers rely on this technology, as do the married couples working in different cities. Relationships are less limited by distance today than in years past. As a result, adults and children have access to each other in unprecedented ways.

Entertainment

Another example of evidence of technological change can be heard in music. Today music is accessible through so many different avenues. Downloaded applications for smart technology number in the hundreds-of-millions. Games, music, videos—you name it—are at people's fingertips wherever they go. Access to the digital marketplace to make purchases has exploded through the years, thanks in large part to Amazon.

Millions of tunes and videos are instantly streamed or digitally available through online and digital stores for smart devices, including iPods, iPhones, Droids, notebooks, and MP3s and MP4s. YouTube and other video and audio formats are wildly popular. Smartphones are now visual and audio entertainment and amusement vaults. Music as well as photos are uploaded and downloaded onto computers. Today, if parents ground children to their rooms, they are technologically *play-grounded*. Therein lies a problem. Children still have access to the outside world. Access to students in the privacy of their own bedrooms is a predator's dream.

The *slow dance* of pseudo-privacy and pseudo-anonymity has begun to ensnare an unwary generation. Some researchers have expressed concern that this relationship between technology and pseudo-privacy has laid groundwork for controversial cultural ideologies and a regular diet of sexual fantasies. This news is not good for our young people online, as each day more stories about immoral teachers and sexual predators abound. The frightening news is the description of the many methods of digital contact by which students place themselves at risk.

Keeping Guards Up

There are many examples of student-to-student and adult-to-student communication crossing all sorts of boundaries. Take, for example, one incident in a

Florida public school: A single, male teacher in his twenties developed an after-hours relationship with several of his female high-school students. His smile was said to melt the hearts of teenage girls, and several had crushes on him.

The teacher and students had been texting each other for months. During this time, a deep attraction emerged between the teacher and one of the girls. He crossed a professional line with a seventeen-year-old student and began spending private time with her after-hours.

To make matters worse, the two of them would appear at games together, only to disappear for several minutes at a time. Parents noticed this and notified administrators. It turned out that the teacher was warned but allowed to stay on the job as long as he changed his behavior. The teacher promised and revised his communication methods. Administrators foolishly believed him.

During one evening school event, the teacher and student were caught alone in one of the classrooms on campus. The girl stated that nothing inappropriate had occurred and that they had just been talking. Suspicions arose when it was learned that the classroom lights had been turned off and the door locked. Cell phone messages and erratic personal behaviors after-hours continued to indicate something was going on between the two, contrary to the student's denial.

The teacher was subsequently placed on administrative leave, and the teenager entered a counseling program to dismantle the emotional bond that had developed between her and the teacher. Stories like these are becoming more and more commonplace and are being reported with greater frequency.

TEACHERS AS SEX SEEKERS

Could it be that teachers and students are having sex today because of a casual, recreational, and consensual desire to explore each other sexually? Are they having sex because they are so desperately in love that they cannot help themselves? Do teachers begin their careers seeking sexual conquests? Each of these questions implies that teachers can be sex seekers.

Education these days is replete with pressures to perform and to continue to meet high standards. Some of the pressures have shifted from academics to social improvements, opening emotions unlike previous decades. It is from within this push for social and emotional improvements that relationship possibilities begin to take shape.

Making condoms available for students to use, to avoid pregnancy by teachers, is unthinkable. Yet on high-school campuses all over this nation, condoms are either available for students who request them or accessible to them with the help of a nurse or counselor.[30] It is now easier for teachers and students, after crossing over boundaries to the point of a physical relationship, to have sex and feel like they are protected.

On a different note, consider the case in Arkansas where a high-school teacher was initially convicted to thirty years in prison for engaging in a sexual relationship with an eighteen-year-old student. The outcome of this case is evidence that a state headed in the wrong direction.

In March 2012, the Arkansas Supreme Court struck down the state's law that banned sexual contact between teachers and students. The court held that people (students) who are eighteen years of age or older have a right to engage in sexual relationships. So long as they are consensual, these relationships in Arkansas are constitutional.

The court took the side of the thirty-eight-year-old David Paschal, an Elkins High School history and psychology teacher. Paschal admitted to having nearly a six-month sexual relationship with one of his eighteen-year-old students. Attorneys for the state argued that the law, which was subsequently overturned by this case, was set in place to protect students from sexual advances from people who are in authority. However, the court found that a sexual relationship between consensual adults was not a crime in Arkansas—regardless of the authority and boundaries between teacher and student.

Writing for the minority opinion, Justice Robert Brown stated that the decision to decriminalize sexual relations between teachers and students would cause disruption in high schools. Teachers could now have sexual relationships with their eighteen-year-old students, and nothing could prevent them from doing so. Here we see our student-centered world now colliding with the world of adult pleasure seekers. This is further evidence of a collapsed morality, another by-product of America's sex culture. Certainly, such experiences are not what states had in mind when they legislated the *whole child education* policy.

Paschal's overturned conviction does not mean that he can return to his job in the classroom. It simply means that he has a right to a sexual relationship with consenting eighteen-year-old students. Now that he is no longer teaching, it makes little difference. What would happen if several states used their ages of consent, versus the age of majority adulthood, for decriminalization of teacher-student sex? There would probably be chaos.

Currently, one-half of the states do not have laws banning teacher-student sex, while some states make it a felony.[31] Our nation needs clear guidelines and enforceable laws that protect students from predators in states that do not ban teacher-student sex. What is to stop a predator teacher from hopping around from state to state, where sex with eighteen-year-olds, or younger, is legal? Simply put, Americans must assume that some adults desire sex with children and are predators. Such adults should not be around children.

America's sex culture has provided an avenue for pedophiles to consider their identity as any other sexual orientation would consider theirs.

Furthermore, pedophilia is quickly becoming acceptable as a valid sexual orientation, along with the accepted homosexuality, lesbianism, and bisexuality orientations. What could be more acceptable to a pedophile than the uncharted sexual territory of a child's first sexual experience? Should a teacher have to admit in an interview before hire or during an annual evaluation that he or she has identified pedophilia as his or her sexual orientation? Some sexual predators make it appear as if they are waiting for legality before they make their move. Others do not wait at all.

Some adults just enjoy teasing about sexual things and leave it at that. Still others boldly proclaim to have as their goal a lifelong commitment with a student and insist that sex is a by-product of the commitment. Sexual relationships are inevitable once the connection passes the point of no return. And technology is right there as a support mechanism for predators in schools, as well as those outside.

The Pleasure Factor

What students find interesting and pleasurable is often not what adults find pleasurable. For example, teenagers may find sensual pleasure tied to fun and social events, because they feel very sexy spending time with people they enjoy and the validating comments they receive. However, if feeling alone and void of deep relationships with peers, performing sex acts with adults may fill a void in their lives because of how deeply personal and *soulish* the act of sex can be.

Providing sex to an older adult could also be akin to playing out a fantasy of desirability, thinking the teacher and the student have a bond so special that no one can share. Likewise, students may view sex with adults through idealism or fantasy, concocted by exposure to peers, and America's ubiquitous sex culture. The problem, though, is that teenage fantasy interests may become teenage fantasies realized, by all-too-willing adult participants. Grooming students is a predator teacher's manipulation, right from the toolbox of tactics. In terms of adults, there are other factors driving these pleasures and may differ between men and women.

Sex as Novelty

In personal discussions with teenagers and their families, it is quite clear that for the male adult seeking sex, once the sex novelty is diminished, so too may be any proclaimed commitment. A teenage conquest may be as much a novelty for an adult as the older person with authority is a novel conquest for the teenager. Adult women seeking sex from teenagers are more inclined to want long-term commitments because their emotional connection through sex is somewhat different from men's. The Letourneau case is a prime example of this type of connection.[32]

Essentially, accounting for the general differences of brains, some present sex for acceptance, while others provide acceptance for sex. The challenge must be for all teachers to analyze their in-person and online connections with their students. They must take a hard look at where any such connections could go in the minds of students. An estimated one-half of high-school students have not had sex. So, of those forming the relationships in question, it is difficult to know whether the sexual bond created is the result of a person becoming sexually active for the first time or the result of a deeper personal connection. The truth is worth repeating: a student does not have to have sex with a teacher for an inappropriate relationship to have occurred.

Could it be that some of our students are losing their virginity to their teachers and experiencing sexual pleasure for the first time? Is this not the epitome of the teacher-student fantasy relationship? If so, the power derived from knowing this is predatory and probably provides an emotional boost to the adult's ego.[33]

PREDATORS GONE WILD

Robert Coles, Harvard psychiatrist and Pulitzer Prize winner, writes:

> Many of the options available to the young come at them not from within (the pressure of instinct, desire, fueling a search for expression) but from without (social and cultural possibilities from a consumerist society ever ready to pester, entice, and seduce an audience and "age group"). Young people . . . take in values from that world, from the music they hear, the movies and television they see, from the fashion, advertising, and magazine industries as they influence what gets worn, what gets said, how hair is cut or colored, what hobbies are pursued.[34]

Many students are ripe for the picking by people who are good at determining when the fruit is ripe. Advertisers know this about consumers. Social media is an emotional fuel for students. Online sexual predators tend to take advantage of loopholes and open doors, when seeking certain types of children and teenagers.[35] A predator teacher would exhibit some of these same tendencies.

Sexual predators desire sexual pleasure through physical contact. They will go to great lengths to secure this contact. Sexual predators do not seek long-term commitments and are not practitioners of lifelong sacrificial love. However, for predators, sexual conquest is also about power—power of mind and heart in order to gain access to the body.

Studies indicate positive correlations between homes with a single parent and a teenager seeking attention from others. As far as the predator is concerned, there is some evidence that also suggests a correlation between adults who were sexually abused as children and the risk they pose for committing similar crimes upon others. That said, the readers must take care so as to not project a simple cause-and-effect relationship between past abuse and future abusive behaviors.[36] That would be unfair and unwise.

When children succumb to adults' psychological manipulation, lusts, and depraved passions, their lives are forever changed. The predator moves from one victim to another in conquest, leaving carnage along the way. Moreover, there is also the possibility that one or more of the children involved do not even consider themselves to have been victimized.

While teacher-student sex may not be enough to define a person as a sexual predator, it is enough in nearly all states to define the teacher's actions as criminal, even requiring some perpetrators to register as sex offenders, lose their teaching license, or both. Students who engage in sexual relationships with their teachers and coaches must come to understand the ramifications of their own actions. They are being victimized by participation and will continue to be victimized by devastating aftereffects, with which they are left to deal.

According Cathy Spatz Wisdom, in an earlier report for the U.S. Department of Justice, through the National Institute for Justice, "Compared to victims of childhood physical abuse and neglect, victims of childhood sexual abuse are at greater risk of being arrested for one type of sex crime: prostitution."[37]

Teachers need to remember that there might be something missing in the lives of students or in the lives of the adults who take advantage of them. But what is missing cannot and must not be found in intimate relationships between the two of them. Relationships with minors are still criminal, and students need protection from those who would manipulate them into a sexual relationship.[38] Again, this is one of the reasons why teachers can be extremely important influences for good in students' lives. But teachers have a high calling and should never forget this truth.

What is it that causes *hyperemotional sexual relationships* between students and their teachers? Aside from the common denominator of academics and the school community, in general, the answer is the same with all close relationships: time spent. These relationships develop by spending more and more personal time together, at school and away from school, as well as in regular communication in off-hours and on vacations.

How this time is spent in a digital age looks very different from even a decade ago. In terms of relationships, teachers must guard against time alone with students, in any personal or professional mode. To do otherwise risks the development of something inappropriate between them.

LET'S GET REAL

Ending this chapter on a positive note will validate all the fine teachers whose motives are pure and whose calling is intact. Teachers' roles have changed over the years. Even so, you won't hear much discussion about this coming from our universities' lecture halls. For example, strategies to develop and nurture vital and appropriate relationships with teenagers are lacking in secondary methods and psychology courses.[39] Philosophy-of-education courses should include the application of philosophy to the building of relationships. It is recommended that courses for teachers-in-training include reflective discussions of the inter-relational philosophies of education and that of the merits public service.

Teachers enjoy normal, healthy relationships across many domains outside of the regular parameters of their employment. They just don't talk about them. Everyone in education is tacitly aware that each relationship means wearing a different hat, depending on the context. But where do teachers form positive relationships outside of class?

Teachers may foster positive relationships with their students and their families by

- attending church where students and families attend;
- coaching a sport or a competitive academic team;
- offering online support for issues outside the scope of understanding of parents through a website developed for a particular class or school program;
- sending regular digital communications about the student's progress; and
- contacting parents when kids are doing well so that the parents can also do well in hearing the teenager's progress.

In terms of the must-haves, in appropriate relationships with students, respect and consistent application of this trait is at the top of the list. High expectations for students, particularly teenage students, mixed with teacher kindness when they mess up are in close second place.[40] Students generally want to be helped to higher standards by their teachers than they usually hold for themselves.

Relationships are nurtured by regular positive and professional communication. Students appreciate those teachers who go out of their way to show they care. In fact, research indicates that students work harder for teachers who genuinely care about them beyond the classroom and have a significant relationship with them than they work for those teachers who don't seem to care as much.[41] Therefore, regular communication between teachers and parents and between teachers and students is essential for healthy teacher-student relationships.

Without transparent communication, a relationship falters. And when unhealthy teacher-student relationships cross the line, there is inevitably more secret communication going on behind the scenes than is evident in the course of the regular school day. In closing, every educator would benefit from this truth: *Transparency, trust, and accountability are three of the beacons that illuminate appropriate relationships.*

SUMMARY

Teachers are too close to students when their proximity is the foundation for serious moral and educational compromises. Proximity compromises occur when teachers' relationships with students (1) distract from the mission of the school, (2) provide emotional confusion for students and teachers, (3) manifest themselves by undercutting or usurping family values of teachers or students, and (4) assume that teachers and students share a very special connection or emotional bond.

Technology and communication from home and in private are the primary enhancements for today's relational bonds. There are three shared traits of inappropriate teacher-student relationships: (1) past abuse, (2) unclear moral compass, and (3) stealth communications. Teachers acting out their sexuality with minors have serious issues, normally stemming from their childhoods. Some of them may have been victims of child sexual abuse, or another form of abuse, during their formative years.

Teachers and students in emotional relationships have unclear moral compasses. Most teenage students are not biologically or emotionally mature enough to have worked out clear moral boundaries. Teachers who lack moral clarity about relationships with students are never to be given daily access to students. A teacher's moral compass is compromised if (1) the teacher has no basis on which to judge whether individual actions are wrong outside of their own beliefs and (2) the teacher acts for self and does not demonstrate concern as to whether anyone else thinks their beliefs and actions are moral.

Teachers who become involved in sexual relationships with students suffer from two flaws in their thinking. The first deals with personal philosophy involving the "exaltation of self," subsequently convincing oneself that he or she is entitled to pursue the course chosen. Flaw number two is illogical, emotional risk-taking. The risk of losing everything for sex with a teenager is illogical. It is also illogical to think a teenage student would stay quiet about such experiences with a teacher.

Technology has changed the nature of relationships in many ways. The possibility of constant communication with others is quite alluring. As each generation has more and more access to communication technologies, people can expect the nature of relationships to continuously change. Teachers who cross into personal relationships with students that eventually incorporate sex use technology as a support mechanism from the beginning.

Not all teachers who have sex with students are predators in the strict definition of the word. After all, a four- or five-year age difference between teacher and student can cause all sorts of emotional confusion. While teacher-student sex may not be enough to define a person as a sexual predator, it is enough in nearly all states to define the teacher's actions as criminal, even requiring the perpetrators to register as a sex offender and lose a teaching license.

DISCUSSION QUESTIONS

1. What are the three factors you would use in determining whether teacher-student relationships are appropriate or not?
2. What is the mission of your school, and in what ways could inappropriate teacher-student relationships compromise this mission?
3. Can you recall any incidents on a local or national level that illustrate the need for a serious discussion or policy change regarding teachers and their relationships with students?
4. Why do you think there are more female teachers being reported and arrested involving sexual relationships with students?
5. What are moral compasses, and how important are they for teachers, students, and parents?
6. What personal factors would motivate a teacher to risk everything for a romantic connection and sexual relationship with a teenage student?
7. As a teacher, or a parent, what is a good general rule to consider when working with students and their friends?
8. What are some characteristics that always seem to appear present when teachers and students engage in inappropriate relationships?
9. If your principal asked you to give a two-minute speech making a case to your colleagues to discuss appropriate and inappropriate relationships, what would you say?
10. What part do communication technologies play in appropriate and inappropriate relationships between teachers and students?

NOTES

1. P. Malatesta. "Teacher faces decades in prison after allegedly having sex with 3 students." *WGN News*. April 5, 2015. Retrieved from https://wgntv.com/2015/04/05/teacher-faces-decades-in-prison-after-allegedly-having-sex-with-3-students/.

2. Charles Montaldo. "Female teachers arrested for having sex with students." *ThoughtCo.* February 12, 2019. Retrieved from https://www.thoughtco.com/female-teachers-arrested-sex-with-students-973219. Cf. Jennifer Preston. "Rules to stop pupil and teacher from getting too social online." *New York Times.* December 17, 2011. Retrieved from www.nytimes.com/2011/12/18/business/media/rules-to-limit-how-teachers-and-students-interact-online.html.

3. Edward F. DeRoche and Mary M. Williams. *Character education: A guide for school administrators.* 2001. Lanham, MD: Scarecrow Press, pp. 68–69.

4. Ernest J. Zarra, III. "Pinning down character education." Summer 2000. *Kappa Delta Pi Record* 36: 4154–157.

5. Richard J. Stiggins, et al. *Classroom assessment for student learning: Doing it right, using it well.* 2009. New York: Allyn and Bacon. Retrieved from www.pbs.org/teacherline/courses/inst325/docs/inst325_stiggins.pdf.

6. Staff. "*Making the case for educating the whole child.*" 2011. Alexandria, VA: Association for Supervision and Curriculum Development. Retrieved from www.wholechildeducation.org/assets/content/mx-resources/WholeChild-MakingTheCase.pdf.

7. Staff. "Love on campus." Summer 2007. *American Scholar* 76(3): 36–46. Retrieved from http://theamericanscholar.org/love-on-campus/.

8. Mikaela Gilbert-Lurie. "Why student-teacher relationships are never OK." *Huffington Post.* April 19, 2012. Retrieved from www.huffingtonpost.com/mikaela-raphael/why-studentteacher-relati_b_1435275.html. Cf. Peggy, AKA Purplmama. "Inappropriate student-teacher relationships, part one," *Hub Pages.* Retrieved from http://purplmama.hubpages.com/hub/Student-Teacher-Relationships-Part-One.

9. K. Boccella, "Inappropriate student-teacher relationships in Lititz." *Philadelphia Inquirer.* May 24, 2009. Retrieved from http://articles.philly.com/2009-05-24/news/24985279_1_warwick-girls-school-board-president-student.

10. Gilbert-Lurie. "Why student-teacher relationships are never OK."

11. Ernest J. Zarra, III. *It should never happen here: A guide to minimizing the risk of child abuse in ministry.* 1997. Grand Rapids, MI: Baker Book House.

12. Paul Thompson, "Teacher accused of having sex with eight pupils on school baseball team faces 20 years in jail." *Mail Online.* June 25, 2008. Retrieved from www.dailymail.co.uk/news/article-1028816/Teacher-accused-having-sex-pupils-school-baseball-team-faces-20-years-jail.html.

13. Zarra, *It should never happen here.*

14. Kelly Babchishin, R. Karl Hanson, and Chantal Hermann. "The characteristics of online sex offenders: A meta-analysis." March 2011. *Sexual Abuse: A Journal of Research and Treatment* 23(1): 92–123.

15. Ibid.

16. Staff. "Teacher-student relationships: How they differ based on student age." *Yahoo Voices.* June 24, 2009. Retrieved from http://voices.yahoo.com/teacher-student-relationships-they-differ-based-3534927.html.

17. Sara G. West, Susan Hatters Friedman, and James L. Knoll IV. "The case of a female teacher who sexually abuses her student: Page 2 of 2." *Psychiatric Times.* April 10, 2012. Retrieved from https://www.psychiatrictimes.com/forensic-psychiatry/case-female-teacher-who-sexually-abuses-her-student/page/0/1.

18. Staff. "Child sexual abuse." March 2011. *American Academy of Child and Adolescent Psychiatry* 9. Retrieved from http://aacap.org/page.ww?name=Child+Sex ual+Abuse&section=Facts+for+Families.

19. Paul E. Mullen and Jillian Fleming. "Long-term effects of child sexual abuse." 1998. *Australian Institute of Family Studies*. Retrieved from https://trove.nla.gov.au/ work/8324208?q&versionId=46377086.

20. D. Finkelhor. "The trauma of child sexual abuse: Two models." 1987. *Journal of Interpersonal Violence* 2: 348–66. Cf. J. Herman, *Trauma and recovery*. 1982. New York: Basic Books.

21. Edward A. Wynne and Kevin Ryan. "Curriculum as a moral educator." *American Educator* Spring 1993, pp.20-24, 43-49. Cf. Kevin Ryan and Karen Bohlin. "Values, views, or virtues." *Education Week*. March 3, 1999. Retrieved from https://www. edweek.org/ew/articles/1999/03/03/25ryan.h18.html.

22. Staff. "Charge: 'Obsessed' teacher raped student." *United Press International*. January 9, 2009. Retrieved from www.upi.com/Top_News/2009/01/09/ Charge_Obsessed_teacher_raped_student/UPI-18641231550223/.

23. Nikki Krize. "Former teacher's aide admits to sex with student." *WNEP*. October 2, 2014. Retrieved from https://wnep.com/2014/10/02/teachers-aide-admits-to-sex-with-student/.

24. Vaishnavi Vaidyanathan. "Teacher had sex with teen student, sent explicit videos through Snapchat." *International Business Times*. September 9, 2019. Retrieved from https://www.ibtimes.com/teacher-had-sex-teen-student-sent-explicit-videos-through-snapchat-2824146.

25. Ibid.

26. Ed Richter, "Female gym teacher accused of sex acts with football players," *Dayton Daily News*. February 8, 2011. Retrieved from www.daytondailynews.com/ news/news/crime-law/female-gym-teacher-accused-of-sex-acts-with-foot-1/nMnx9/.

27. Staff. "Anthony Alvarez, former Arvada High School assistant principal, arrested for alleged sexual relationship with 15-year-old student." *Huffington Post*. September 6, 2011. Retrieved from www.huffingtonpost.com/2011/09/06/anthony-alvarez-former-ar_n_950907.html.

28. "Narcissistic personality disorder." *Psychology Today*. September 16, 2019 Retrieved from www.psychologytoday.com/conditions/narcissistic-personality-disorder.

29. Alan K. Goodboy and Scott A. Myers. "Human communication: A publication of the Pacific and Asian Communication Association." *Semantic Scholar*. 2008. 11(3): 341–56.

30. Carolyn Kuimelis. "Schools should provide free condoms to students." *The Oracle*. October 11, 2016. Retrieved from https://gunnoracle.com/9099/uncategorized/ schools-should-provide-free-condoms-to-students/. Cf. Mark A. Schuster, Robert M. Bell, Sandra H. Berry, et al. "Impact of a high school condom availability program on sexual attitudes and behaviors." March/April 1998. *Perspectives on Sexual and Reproductive Health* 30(2): 67–72.

31. Alan K. Goodboy and Scott A. Myers. "Arkansas court rules teachers can have sexual relationship with of-age students." *CBS News*. March 30, 2012.

Retrieved from http://stlouis.cbslocal.com/2012/03/30/ark-court-rules-teachers-can-have-sexual-relationship-with-of-age-students/.

32. Lisa Habib. "Why do teens have sex? For intimacy, social status, study says." *WebMD*. June 14, 2006. Retrieved from www.foxnews.com/story/0,2933,199540,00.html.

33. Sabrina Weill. *The real truth about teens and sex*. 2005. New York: Perigee Books/Penguin. See also Sabrina Weill. "The real truth about teens and sex." *CBS News*. August 15, 2012. Retrieved from www.cbsnews.com/2100-500186_162-831562.html.

34. Robert Coles. *The moral intelligence of children*. 1997. New York: Random House Publishers, p. 164.

35. Abbie Alford. "Social media fueling teacher and student relationships." *Fox News*. May 23, 2012. Retrieved from www.fox23.com/mostpopular/story/Social-media-fueling-teacher-student-sexual/pol.

36. Alex Brown. "Experts explain the beginnings of inappropriate student-teacher relationships." *WIBC News*. May 11, 2012. Retrieved from www.wibc.com/news/story.aspx?ID=1702145.

37. Cathy Spatz Wisdom. "Victims of childhood sexual abuse: Later criminal consequences." *National Institute of Justice: U.S. Department of Justice Research Brief*. March 1995. Retrieved from https://www.ncjrs.gov/pdffiles/abuse.pdf.

38. Zarra. *It should never happen here.*

39. R. Miller and J. Pedro. "Creating respectful classroom environments." 2006. *Early Childhood Education* 33(5):293–99.

40. Mary Ann Ware and Jodi Rath. "4 must-haves for positive teacher-teen relationships." *Association for Supervision and Curriculum Development*. May 9, 2019. Vol. 14, No. 26. Retrieved from http://www.ascd.org/ascd-express/vol14/num26/4-must-haves-for-positive-teacher-teen-relationships.aspx. Cf. Jody Marberry. "Here's what teens say they need." *Association for Supervision and Curriculum Development*. May 9, 2019. Vol. 14, No. 26. Retrieved from http://www.ascd.org/ascd-express/vol14/num26/heres-what-teens-say-they-need.aspx.

41. J. A. Hall-Lande, M E. Eisenberg, S. L. Christenson, et al. "Social isolation, psychological health, and protective factors in adolescence." 2006. *Adolescence* 42(166): 265–86.

Chapter 5

Relationships and Social Networking in a Digital World

I think social media has taken over for our generation. It's a big part of our lives, and it's kind of sad.

—Kendall Jenner

Two of the more commonly used terms that refer to communications technology focus on relational aspects. The general term *social networking* most commonly refers to the actions of using technology to connect with other people on several interpersonal and intersocial levels. The term *social network* pertains to the actual components of the technology, as well as groups established by relationships. Humans often use technology for social purposes and "depend on social interaction for their constitution."[1] Students use technology for three main purposes: (1) social interaction, (2) entertainment and leisure, and (3) school requirements.

Facebook, WhatsApp, Instagram, SnapChat, TikTok, Pinterest, and LinkedIn are examples of online social networking communities. There are also video communities such as YouTube, GodTube, Vimeo, and still others, along with sites like Twitter and Parler—as well as the untold number of interactive online gaming sites. Also part of the social networking scene online are adult sites, dating and sex sites, and relationship and marriage-seeking sites. Whatever it is one seeks with another human being can be found somewhere on the Internet, either on the World Wide Web, Deep Web, or the Dark Web.[2]

All social networking communities operate on the fundamental premise that their mission is to connect people with ease, and to do so as seamlessly as possible. The social sites are largely successful at accomplishing their mission—and sometimes too successful. The foci in this chapter are the social connections made through communication technologies, as these affect teacher-student relationships.[3]

TECHNOLOGY AND INCREASED RISK

Teachers and students live under enormous pressures to demonstrate successful outcomes of their teaching and of student learning. Technology is supposed to assist with classroom instruction, data and record-keeping, and provide measurement of student and school outcomes. For some schools, technology has become a source of distraction to learning. Additional pressures are added by local communities, which clamor for excellence among students in academics, athletics, and activities. The media hop on almost any story that deals with schools. And nothing gets a community's attention like a scandal involving teachers and students.

Everyone who has access to technology could now look up just how well, or poorly, their children's schools are performing. Schools are still rated and ranked for their academic performance. But they are also ranked accordingly to a host of other criteria.

The communication gap between many schools and their stakeholders has closed precipitously. One of the downsides to this closeness is the formation of snap judgments, often based on a pie chart or set of statistical data.

In the early to mid-1990s, few students had cell phones on school campuses, and personal computers were gaining popularity. A parent would phone or maybe e-mail a teacher to see how a student was performing. Many pieces of school literature were mailed home via the U.S. Postal Service. Today, schools would be hard-pressed to find their employees and student without smartphones. Why should this be an added concern for schools?

Smartphones Are Life

What is it about technology that brings students their sense of identity? Students have this sense of feeling lost if they do not have access to their devices for just a few minutes. The easy answer is because their device is their immediate gratification for curiosity and their primary mode of socialization. Both connectivity and socialization are the focal points of teenage psyches and adults too, for that matter. There is a similarity between an addict's substance and people having to check in on social media, as this chapter will point out. The possessiveness that people exhibit over their smart devices is tantamount to relational intimacy, without which personal identity is diminished. Adults are sometimes scarcely better.

How many teachers have asked students in classes to end a phone call only to have the student reply, "It's my mom?" Some students use smartphones to invade privacy. In addition, students also have recorded teachers after baiting them in class. Through correspondence with teachers from around the nation, and some international correspondence, there is the sense that smartphone policy enforcement is a lost cause. Phones are too personalized these days and too much a part of students' lives. And it doesn't end there, as adults feel the same way. In fact, teachers are probably some of the worst violators.[4]

Smartphones are not only the identities of students. Families have their own group identities, as well. In terms of practical usage, students inform their parents almost instantly about things that occur on campus. Whether a student wins an election, wants to go home for the day, or is upset over personal circumstances, they have instant encouragement and empathy. They also prompt parents' emotional reactions with parts of stories that somehow place the students in the best light, which usually blow up over time.

If a student is in tears over a grade, he finds a way within seconds to text his parents, who, within minutes, are either on the phone or sending an e-mail to a number of addresses. In reality, students are not being held to any serious account for their participation in the very communications culture that encircles them. This extends also to connecting with teachers. In the minds of some educators, child-centered education includes their access to their technology to meet their academic, social, and emotional needs, and it also means access to them.

One interesting thing about this is that some school campuses across the nation have policies that smartphones are not to be on or used throughout the school day. Yet the tempting power of the smartphone these days is astounding.[5] The following three interesting facts illustrate these points.

1. The Pew Research Center has determined that teenagers exchange an average of sixty-seven text messages a day.[6] Overall, Americans send roughly 26 billion text messages per day.[7]
2. In some states, like Minnesota, there are suicide hotlines set up for troubled teenagers and others who are desperate and need someone to text. The number of text messages is equivalent to the number of actual phone calls received prior to the text hotline.[8]
3. An estimated 75 percent of high-school-aged teenagers have cell phones. Girls tend to text more, with fourteen- to seventeen-year-olds sending more than one hundred texts a day. According to Pew, teenagers talk to their friends by text message. However, they are much more likely to use voice contact with their parents via cell phone.[9]

TEACHERS ON EGGSHELLS

Many teachers recall when it was acceptable for students to be personally challenged to become more responsible and to work harder. Parents today are less supportive of teachers and schools than they are of their children. Some students claim teachers are picking on them when they confront their work ethic issues. Parents are usually quick to defend their child over the teacher, especially when only one side of a conflict is presented to them. All a teacher has to do today is to remove a student's phone from him or her and watch how the attacks unfold. Some teachers are assaulted by students because of actions like these.

Any form of criticism in today's culture is often taken as badgering and unkind. Students and parents perceive most forms of school or classroom discipline as personal attacks. In retaliation to these perceived attacks, negative comments are posted. Communication technologies are presenting new concerns for schools. It is concerning because of the need for some people to *weaponize* the medium to their advantage.

There is the tendency today for parents to go over the teacher's head to the principal or even above the principal to the district office and avoid face-to-face resolution. Technology and e-mail links mean board presidents and superintendents' offices are a mere click away. Impulsive vents and angry diatribes are received every day by colleagues across this nation. Parents see the ease of adopting a model of *confrontation without confronting*. There is simplicity in using technology to access those in authority.

This approach can be hazardous to reputations and to employment. The fact is that people are more inclined to draft something in text or writing they probably would not say to a person face to face. There is a perceived power of the keyboard. Once these types of messages are received, teachers are wary about their relationships with parents and take extra care around them. This cannot help but affect students.

Beware the Befriending

The social networking that occurs from home can become problematic for even the more seasoned online veterans. Some teachers are part of this network and enjoy it. Others find nothing but potential drama and avoid it. The following is an example of online social media drama, offering a few reasons why some teachers choose to avoid social media platforms and connecting with parents and students altogether.

Interest begins with an innocent set of exchanges on Facebook. Married and single teachers begin *friending* current and past students and open their personal lives to them while away from work. Teachers *liking* students. Students *liking* teachers. It is genuine and fun and the interactions are applauded by students as authentic.

Conversely, what starts out as innocent turns into what some misconstrue as teasing and flirtatious remarks. Photos are posted and comments made about the photos. Copies of photos are circulated, and some are changed through digital software programs and then reposted, for what appears to be fun. However, students' fun at the disposal of a teacher's reputation amounts to only one-sided fun that eventually amounts to bullying. Students follow posts closely, copy some exchanges, and pass them around. Like wildfire, rumors of on-campus affairs between teachers, students, and administrators are spread around to the hundreds involved in their online community.

Like clockwork, some parents, who are part of the network of online friends, take it upon themselves to copy and paste some of the posts and chats and forward them to the school district officials and school board members. Some teachers are questioned and even asked to delete their online profiles. All of this leads to the fundamental query: *Where are the common sense district guidelines for teachers during their off-hours, as they pertain to connecting socially with students and parents?*

How Social Is Too Social?

The online world is full of emotions and imaginations—a world where many cyberspace answers are multiple choice and advice aplenty. In this online world, there are few incorrect responses. Hara Estroff Marano explains how this world can ensnare the unaware:

> An extraordinary number of people spend an extraordinary amount of time online connecting with other people. They reveal their deepest, darkest secrets to folks who may be strangers, and they often find these relationships so compelling they seem more emotionally real and alive than the marriages they are actually in. Indeed, online relationships can be unusually seductive. They are readily accessible, they move very quickly, and under the cloak of anonymity they make it easy for people to reveal a great deal about themselves.
>
> Putting themselves into words, getting replies while they're still in the emotional state of the original message, relying heavily on imagination to fill in the blanks about the recipient, people communicating online are drawn into such rapid self-disclosure that attachments form quite literally with the speed of light.[10]

Each new generation of technology obviously brings with it many concerns. The fact that more teachers and students spend significant time getting to know the other does have merits. At the same time, these developing relationships have prompted more than a little attention. School districts are asking themselves how social is too social for their teachers and what is an appropriate depth for these developing relationships?

Districts are also pondering what is best to do about after-hours communications while teachers are on their own time. For example, if a teacher posts a rude comment on a social networking site, on their own time, who is liable for the offensive statements? Are such statements enough to release a teacher from his or her contract? What about material that appears in joke form? Are there any district-level expectations that extend beyond the contractual day if a person online is a teacher, coach, or even an administrator from a particular school?

What happens when students become emotionally and intimately involved online with their teachers? Are the students corrected or disciplined for taking matters too far? Recent reviews of large high school-district websites indicate that there is some movement toward establishing general policy guidelines concerning employees and their use of district-provided communication technologies. These pertain to the contract day, and since unions are involved, it is difficult to hold teachers to anything that occurs on their own time. Also, the constraints will only apply to us of district-assigned, or district-provided technology, Wi-Fi, or any smart devices. How can a district hold a teacher liable for personal use of his or her own technology on school time?

No one knows what actual constraints will be placed upon individual administrators, teachers, counselors, and coaches. However, in a performance-based environment such as schools, which are also highly social environments, school-district employees should sit up and take notice. Advocating for and taking the high road is often best in such environments. Steering clear of anything that smacks of inappropriateness is the high road and one that is best for students and teachers in the end.

This is the direction that the Los Angeles Unified School District (LAUSD) took in February 2012 as it released its first-ever social media policy. The preference of the LAUSD is that there be no interaction between teachers and students on Facebook, for example, except through professional accounts, which is distinct from any student and teacher personal account, page, or website. The 41,000 student Kern High School District in Kern County, California, has adopted a similar policy, as have the New York City public schools.[11]

Inappropriate Texting

As gratifying as immediate contacts are to the psyche, there are some cautions that arise with them. The chances of texting something that could be misconstrued or inappropriate rise in proportion to one's automatic impulsivity. Rapid communication of ideas as one-liners and images is just drama waiting to happen in the high-hormone, high-tech world of communication technologies.

At first glance, text exchanges between teachers and students might seem quite innocent. It would not take long for a brief chat to move into a more relaxed round of texts. Therefore, what begins innocently can be diminished in a flash. There are at least three reasons for this. *First*, students and teachers have each other's personal cell numbers and they are communicating during school and during off-hours. *Second*, it becomes very easy to begin teasing and flirting in text, which can lead to misunderstandings quickly. *Third*, teachers should seriously consider any text or online exchange as a moment which might eventually compromise his or her family or employment.

The fact that a teacher could not recognize the direction of a chat means the teacher's moral compass switch had been disabled for a short time. However, if the teacher's moral compass was working correctly and still allowed a compromising exchange, this also becomes a concern. The fact is then both the teacher and the student crossed a line.

In the real world, when inappropriate incidents occur, the outcomes are much harsher and often more dramatic. Take, for example, the following text message exchange shown to administrators by a female student. The following verbatim, last text message exchange occurred during a class session.[12]

Teacher: I'm focused on you. U think I wanna risk my livelihood? You sitting next to me right now is making me feel so erotic.

Student: Look, I think u shud stop textin me bcuz u r making me so uncomfortable. U have a wife and 2 kids 2 b focused on.

Teacher: But I really wanta date u, after u graduate. U have never answered how you feel about me.

Student: I don't feel that way abt u. ur my teacher. I cnt tell bcuz im not focused on dat trying 2 complete my assignment so u wnt give me an F.

After the female student shared the text message exchange with school administrators, they took immediate action and fired the teacher. A reexamination of the police records showed the teacher who was fired had several past misdemeanors—and even an arrest for indecent exposure. However, these did not show up on the teacher's state background check.

The ease at which this exchange occurred should bring all teachers and parents to full attention. These types of exchanges happen more often than parents are aware.[13] Teachers must remember their calling and position and stay far away from these exchanges with students. There can be no compromise on this. Teachers remain public figures with positions of authority over children.

Easy Access

Technology makes it easier to stay in touch with others and makes it easy to say things that are not appropriate. Thirty-nine-year-old Oregon charter-school director Michael Bremont discovered this to be the case. He began texting a sixteen-year-old female student after-hours, which then led to flirtation. Over time, Bremont went too far, and a close sexual relationship developed. He was arrested for sodomy, attempted rape, and sexual abuse.[14]

There are obviously times when communicating with students after-hours is appropriate. However, as the readers have noticed, even texting students is risky. Even with the purest of motives, message exchanges can take on a life of their own and are permanent records of moments in time, which are sometimes blown up to become larger than life.

Parents and students have real-time access to academic progress, attendance data, work missed, and grades. Smartphone applications are available for students to access their own grades and academic portfolios. Text messaging is a part of many school districts' emergency alert systems, as well as personalized classroom updates.

Students pressure themselves to participate in a variety of exhausting extracurricular activities, not to mention later applying to numerous colleges and for many scholarships as high-school students. Teachers aren't immune from the hectic pace and are now on call throughout the day when parents want to know why their teenager earned a poor score on an exam. But all of these routines can change in a flash, and technology can become a source of heartache and ruination.

Shock waves ripple across the nation when Americans hear of the horrific incidents of bullying that take place in schools. Social media often brings valid attention to these incidents.[15] There should be no rush to judgment that teachers who flirt with students are sexual predators. However, it can be argued that all teacher-student sexual relationships generate after-hours flirtation and sex talk and videos almost always are recorded on someone's smart device. It is merely the nature of the *sex culture beast*, if you will. This is the reason law enforcement officials issue warrants at the point of arrest to seize computers, cell phones and cell phone records, and other personal devices. For the record, sensual teasing, or what most consider flirtation, should be completely off-limits between teachers and students.

TEACHER-STUDENT ONLINE COMMUNICATION TEST

Teachers can avoid many of the Internet's thorniest concerns with students if they apply certain principles to their time online. As an example of one of these principles, teachers should reflect on the application of their actions with the suggested *Teacher-Student Online Communication Test*, found in table 5.1.

Table 5.1   Teacher-Student Online Communication Test

Teachers at all levels. . .
We must always remember that we are dealing with other persons' children.
Therefore. . .
We must walk in the shoes of the parents, asking ourselves whether our behaviors with students would be appropriate and acceptable to us if the situation were different, involving a colleague and one of our own children.

Illustration of the larger point is found in a confrontation once had with a local journalist. The journalist insisted that society makes too much out of issues concerning sex. He had written an article in support of a friend who had been arrested for soliciting a prostitute for sex while on vacation in San Francisco. His friend had *hooked up* via the Internet with a supposed female escort, who turned out to be a law enforcement officer.

The journalist argued that prostitution should be legal and that women who chose that as a career should have every right to do so. The journalist is not alone in calling for legalizing sex work. Some physicians and college professors are calling for the same thing.[16]

The look on the journalist's face was priceless when I asked whether he had any children and specifically any daughters in his family. He responded that he did and that he had one daughter. Furthermore, when asked whether it would be acceptable to him if his daughter came home one day to announce she had discovered her life's calling at age seventeen, and that she had a part-time internship in-training to become professional sex worker, and escort, there was silence.

There is a basic moral lesson to be gleaned from this anecdote. When it comes to our own children, we are less likely to support someone else's immorality, as our own and for our own. This principle applies to the ways teachers view colleagues' actions toward the teacher's own children. This also raises a larger question, as parents are concerned about their own children spending time pondering other people's immorality.

Parents do not desire their children to be exposed and exploited online, especially in this age of permanent digital storage and retrieval. Too bad more teachers do not stop to consider this basic moral consideration as parents.

PRINCIPLES FOR APPROPRIATE
AFTER-HOURS COMMUNICATION

Teachers who either find they are required to communicate with their teenage students after school hours or have an extended interest in staying in touch with students—including at-risk students—would benefit from guidelines for appropriate behavior. When done correctly, such communication can be a positive and impacting extension of the classroom, as well as a reinforcement of professional and respectful boundaries.

Teachers as Buddies

Adults should carefully consider the environments in which they choose to hang out with teenagers, especially those where control and respect are more socially relaxed. For example, a coach or a teacher can maintain control of the environment after basketball practice in the gym or talking informally about school, homework, or the next game. However, this same conversation within a more relaxed context takes on another different level of communication.

Controlled environments are the classrooms, at lunch, or after school, where doors are unlocked and traffic can enter rooms at any time. These are typical protocols when teachers and student are meeting. There should be no compromise of professionalism, regardless the environment. These and other protocols encourage safety within *Student and Faculty Environments*. Schools must regularly emphasize such protocols.

Spending one-on-one time with a teenage student, grabbing a coffee at a local shop, or enjoying a friendly get-together over current students is riskier. There is nothing inherently wrong with such meetings. But risk increases each time a teacher moves outside the professional academic or school-related activity regimen. What exactly is the risk? The risk is that the teacher steps down to the level of that of a friend. Taking this risk and elevating it with the addition of friendly, private communication as friends raises the risk even more. Camaraderie should never replace professionalism and conversation should be guarded, so as not to violate the trust parents have placed on the teacher.

Things to Consider

Teachers and students who draw closer than they should run the risk of rumors and reputational questions. As a result, teachers are instructed never to use phrases such as "I like you" or to make up private pet names when dealing one on one with students. Sensual or sexual teasing is always inappropriate. If anything is learned from the cases related throughout this book, it must be that teachers should never engage in flirtation or provide for flirtatious openings with students.

Teachers must be above reproach and never lead students on sensually or emotionally. Ignoring this basic common sense is to ignore boundaries. Ignoring boundaries is the first overstep down the path that has proven destructive to so many teachers. In addition to guarding against flirtation with students, teachers have another consideration: inappropriate language, such as profanity, sexual innuendo, or urban phrases. One of the common denominators discovered in teacher-student emotional and physically intimate relationships is the use of such language.

A SAFER APPROACH

A highly recommended professional and personal social media ethic is for teachers to have no students on any of their personal social media pages. The risk is greater when students are given access to personal photos, a teacher's adult friends and family, and join in the relaxed context in which protocols of employment are routinely dismissed. A good general rule is that any student asking to be part of a teacher's personal network must first be a former student and have graduated from high school or college. Even then, there are risks, due to age or gender gaps.

Most of what a current student needs to share with a teacher can be posted on a professional page or even wait until the next morning at school. Teachers should not *need* to communicate socially with students or through a website outside of the work server. Learning from others' mistakes means teachers should simply not place themselves in risky situations when it comes to their communications and professional relationships with students and parents. All it takes is one misunderstanding for an allegation of impropriety to work against a teacher's credibility and reputation. There are plenty of examples where this is exactly the outcome.

I'm Sexy, and I Show It!

There is a groupthink among a certain cadre of online users that sometimes anonymity equals impunity. The sense of power that comes with technology feeds many egos, from which few are exempt. Sometimes a computer empowers people to feel sexy or cool, all within the confines of a controlled environment. The reality is that, regardless of the age, people want others to notice them, to like them, and to admire them. Teachers must guard against this temptation, especially when it comes to work and developing a realistic sense of security while using the Internet for social reasons.

Elias Aboujaoude, a clinical assistant professor in psychiatry and behavioral sciences at Stanford University, confirms that "although studies show that more than 160 million Americans are regular Internet users, little research has been conducted on problematic Internet use. . . . A 2002 study in the journal *Cyber Psychology & Behavior* found that 60 percent of companies surveyed had disciplined, and more than 30 percent had terminated, employees for inappropriate Internet use."[17]

Some colleagues envision a time when such discipline is meted out to those in education, as a result of teachers' poor choices. However, what would that do to an already-depleted core of public school educators? There can be little doubt that with today's smartphones teachers and students upload data to social media sites while *on the clock*. Absence of district and school policy could bring legal trouble. Some districts find this risk an acceptable one. Conversely, the existence of policy and subsequent violation could bring disciplinary action.[18]

TEACHER-PARENT RELATIONSHIPS

If daily news headlines are accurate, then there are serious issues emerging between teachers and parents as they are interacting more and more on social networking sites. The very first rule that teachers should apply is *never post anything on any social networking sites that you do not mind being seen by your friends, your friends of friends, your family, and even strangers*. Teachers are public figures and are sometimes both parents of their colleagues' children and of their own, as students. What is posted becomes quite permanent somewhere and can lead to fractured relationships between adults and colleagues, alike.

People download and save so much from the Internet that the exercise of restraint toward what we post online is most prudent. Even while joking, the embellishing of either semi-true or fictional accounts that are analogous to real people may be taken more seriously than intended. Teachers need to be careful of those who practice the *gotcha* mentality. Not everyone will like their children's teachers. Likewise, teachers and parents should always remind themselves that the freedom of expression is not absolute and that people can sue others for whatever appears offensive or feels like a threat.

Today, most parents and teachers have access to each other on school-related academic Internet sites. As a result, there are instances where socializing online may be appropriate. Appropriate use of social technology respects the two levels of relationships. As a reminder to teachers and parents, when posting on social networking sites, avoid making statements about students, programs, teachers, and achievement. Posts affirming positive things create a friendly environment for others to post the same. Also, there should never be created anonymous or *fake* profiles, doxing of someone, or digging for information to use against another. Those antics only lead to trouble. Who can forget the 2008 case of Lori Drew, a mother who assisted others in the creation of a fake teenage boy's MySpace page?

The sole purpose of Drew's MySpace page was to form a romantic bond with a teenage girl at her daughter's school and then dump her for everyone to see the falling-out. The victim, Megan Meier, was prone to depression and after the incident committed suicide, having been told by Lori Drew and others, "The world would be a better place without you." Remember to keep it positive, cordial, jovial, and lighthearted.[19] If there is a major issue that needs to be addressed, parents should make appointments with the teacher to meet in person.

Working Together

Teachers and parents must understand that actions online may have implications long after the computer is powered down for the evening. The last thing any teacher or parent needs before retiring for the night is a chemically charged-up brain with negative emotions, by reading comments related to personal things written or shared, even in jest. Parents strive to guard their children from this and the concern should also be valid for adults.

Together, teachers and parents can affect substantive change, as they forge appropriate and positive relationships. In building capital with parents, teachers must take extra care to remain as professional as possible. The development of relationships between teachers and parents should be developed with no less concern.

Communication is the key to working relationships. Therefore, in these working relationships, keeping parents in the communications loop is essential. This can be done on appropriate relational levels, and here is where technology can be a terrific tool.

Table 5.2 illustrates two self-explanatory, appropriate relational levels for teachers and parents as they network to build overall educational relationships.[20] With the latter in mind, three questions are presented for the readers' consideration.

Table 5.2   Two Levels of Teacher-Parent Networking Relationships

Level 1: Professional-Academic Relationships
- Students are the focal point.
- Data and complete information about academic progress and achievement are characteristics of this level.
- This represents the academic, classroom side of the relationship.
- In an ideal educational world, this is a relationship that all teachers should have with parents.

Level 2: Interpersonal Activity-Based Relationships
- This includes nonschool-related activities and usually occurs away from the school site.
- This also includes academics in terms of competitions, athletic events, booster-club fundraisers, school-site councils, church, civic involvement, and political participation.
- Interpersonal relationships exist when teachers and parents work together in areas that are not strictly tied to academics at the school.

1. Should teachers and parents date and subsequently form personal relationships, during any time they are working together and sharing the common responsibility of educating a student?
2. What are the chances of special privileges being granted to *favorite* students and developing a conflict of interest?
3. Is it appropriate for teachers to befriend parents on social networking sites, like Facebook, WhatsApp, SnapChat, TikTok, and others, and talk freely about life and work, including on video cams?

What about Dating?

Americans consider themselves quite sophisticated, and the mere notion of moderation of adult relationships is deemed preposterous by some. Colleagues scoff at the notion and reply with the usual retort: *What I do on my on time and with whom is my business.* To some extent, this is exactly correct. However, it is to the advantage of the teacher to point out that what teachers do on their own time with parents of their students must be considered in another. That is, there is the risk of developing a conflict of interest.

What begins as casual could easily spill over into the classroom. Comments from students, colleagues, and from other parents in the community may creep into the school and affect the focus and mission of the teacher. The fact is that any issues that would arise between a parent and a teacher would probably find their ways onto the Internet. Subsequently, what was meant as private would then be no longer regarded as such. When it comes to dating parents, teachers must always place the students and their callings as teachers over the adult relationships formed, in order to avoid issues down the line.

Teachers who live in communities where schools are more neighborhood-oriented are much more likely to cross paths out in public with students and parents from their schools. Whether at a mall, a movie theater, grocery store, church, or sporting events, it is a fact that people's paths cross within communities. Sometimes teachers and parents work together on events that are political or perhaps a fundraiser for a charity. People network over a variety of causes and concerns and teachers must be aware that their reputations are not only present in the minds of the students but also realities for their parents.

Conflicts occur on all school campuses. Therefore, teachers must seek to minimize these conflicts when they can. If one such conflict arises out of a failing relationship a teacher has with one of his or her student's parents, then complications arise which affect the student and the conflict inflates beyond the control of the teacher.

The Special Privilege Relationship

There are students and athletes with whom teachers have certain affinities. Shared interests or shared responsibilities enable some personalities to just *click*. Humans are social creatures and developing friendships is often a matter of finding those with whom we have things in common. Parents find that they might have a closer relationship with one of their children than with the others in the family. When it comes to teachers and coaches, caution needs to be applied in these cases of feeling immediate connections.

No one needs an allegation of special treatment of one student over another or unfair treatment of one player over another. As a coach, players should sense fairness in treatment extended to all players. As a teacher, there should be no special privilege granted to one student over another.

Beware the Unexpected

Some students feel more attached to their former teacher than the teachers realize. The author's own personal experience revealed that his classroom instructional and relational time made a difference well into the future.

Back in 1999, a student phoned me at home. I happened to be in, so I answered, asking with whom I was speaking.

A younger male voice said, "You know who I am. You were my teacher a few years ago."

"Oh, all right," I said, moving the conversational pleasantries right along, when I was abruptly interrupted.

"Zarra," the caller said, "I have a gun to my head, and I going to kill myself tonight. Before I do, I wanted to talk to someone I thought cared about me and my life."

Stunned, I somehow managed to calmly say, "May I ask your name, please?"

He declined to tell me. To his credit, he did offer that he was high from smoking marijuana, so I was aware of his mental and emotional states. In short order, I was able to get law-enforcement on another line to help me, all while continuing to talk with the young man. Luckily, in the end things worked out all right, as I was able to assure the young man I would be able to find help for him.

As a busy teacher, and not at work, I could have chosen several courses of action when I received my former student's call for help. I quickly realized my role as former teacher was not as his lecturer that evening. I was reminded that students see their teachers differently throughout their lives, as they move on into adulthood. Yet, somehow, we always remain their *teachers*. As teacher, I was not compensated to counsel or talk with former students or those who are under the influences of drugs. Yet when he called and explained his predicament, the images in my head were as compelling as they were inescapable. If that had been my child, I would have wanted someone to take the time to help.

In sharing this personal example, I hope to demonstrate what many educational researchers are discovering about relationships between teachers and teenage students: students saying they have relationships at school with their teachers is very different from saying that they know their teachers will go the extra mile for them. Teachers being friendly and professional are highly respected by many parents and students. Often, this respect has to be realized over time and through demonstrative actions.

There is nothing extraordinary about my story. Other teachers step into the gap to assist as the needs present themselves. Sometimes teachers are the recipients of only negative press. The fact is when teachers show profound concern, they necessarily touch the lives of their students in myriad ways beyond the classroom.[21] As a result, doing so forms vital and unique relationships with students' parents, too.

Speaking with many teachers over the years and listening to their personal anecdotes affirms that students and families respond better to the school when appropriate relationships are a significant part of the education process for their teenagers. Education is a people profession. The parents of the suicidal young man who called me ended up being very glad a former teacher took the time to talk their son down from a drug-induced, escalated emotional crisis. Many teachers choose to involve themselves in similar crises because they have taken the time to form meaningful relationships with their students along the way. And many hurting students turn to teachers in the first place because of these nurturing, healthy relationships.

MORE RESEARCH NEEDED

Past education research on teacher-student relationships focused on student learning outcomes and teacher efficacy. The effects of the relationships were correlated to various assessments, including literacy scores, high-school exit-exam scores, teacher stress measurement, and student self-efficacy. Meta-analyses conclude that teachers have tremendous impact on student learning, both positively and negatively, and that these relationships matter.[22]

Wubbels has made some inroads by examining the teacher behaviors in these relationships. He concludes, "Two decades of research on teacher-student relationships in class" focuses on "teaching from an interpersonal perspective using a communicative systems approach and propos[ing] a model to describe teacher-student relationships in terms of teacher behavior."[23]

In a British study Salzberger-Wittenberg et al. asked "whether students' misbehavior had been consistently linked . . . to teachers' reports of stress." The authors speculated as to whether or not "teacher stress, negative affect, and self-efficacy predict the quality of student-teacher relationships."[24] Lately, there are more and more studies that examine the emotional and physical relationships that develop between students and teachers. Maybe it is time to involve the parent-teacher relationships as well.

SUMMARY

The general term *social networking* refers to using technology to connect with other people. The term *social network* can pertain to the actual components of the technology, among other things. Technology increases access points for all education stakeholders and continues to enable that certain instantaneous communication remains the norm.

Smartphones are teenagers' lives! The phone is their immediate gratification and mode of socialization with many others, simultaneously. It is equivalent to having a built-in audience at one's disposal.

In most middle and secondary schools, cell-phone-policy enforcement is a losing battle. Other nations also struggle with cell-phone-policy enforcement. There is no turning back. Phones are too personalized these days and too much a part of students' lives to be removed.

There are obviously many concerns surrounding the online world. School districts are questioning how social is too social for their teachers and administrators. Teachers must remember their calling and position does not change because they are away from the classroom. The physical presence of an adult with a teenager is no longer necessary for abuse to occur in student's lives. Americans are shocked by the horrific incidents of bullying that take place in schools from within the digital world. Parents and teenagers are sometimes caught up in social frenzies. Social media often plays roles in these phenomena.

Most American parents care about the education their teenagers receive. Therefore, teachers and their teenage students' parents forming personal relationships run the risk of conflicts of interest. The implications are many if there is a falling out in the relationship. Campus spirit is affected. The classroom is affected. The spreading of rumors distracts from the educational focus on the school.

Relationships in the digital realm are as real as relationships that are in the flesh. Teachers and parents must understand that actions online, for more than professional reasons, may have implications long after the computer is shut down for the evening.

DISCUSSION QUESTIONS

1. What are some ways that social networking can positively enhance professional and healthy relationships between teachers and students?
2. Why are teenagers in high schools so attached to their smartphones?
3. Considering the power of information and connection possibilities that exist with smartphones today, what are some ways teachers can harness this power for use in the classroom?
4. How social is too social for teachers in relation to students and parents?
5. What are your district's policies about teachers and students using personal devices on campus?
6. If your district superintendent asked you to present to the school board your best case as to why there should be either (1) an easing of on-campus cell phone restrictions or (2) a tightening of on-campus cell phone restrictions, what would your presentation include?
7. What guidelines should exist for communications and relationships between teachers and students during off-hours?
8. What is the importance of a reflective teacher-student online communication test?
9. Has your school developed principles for appropriate after-hours communications and relationships between students and teachers?
10. What are the key factors to keep in mind during the development of *appropriate* parent-teacher relationships?

NOTES

1. Maarten Derksen and Anne Beaulieu. "Social technology." July 2012. *The Sage Handbook of the Philosophy of Social Sciences*. October 27, 2019. Retrieved from www.virtualknowledgestudio.nl/documents/_annebeaulieu/5579-Jarvie-Chap37.pdf.

2. Steve Symanovich. "How to safely access the deep and dark webs." *Symantec Corporation*. 2019. Retrieved from https://us.norton.com/internetsecurity-how-to-how-can-i-access-the-deep-web.html.

3. Ferris Jabr. "Insights: The new rules of social networking." *Psychology Today* November/December 2008, pp. 5–16.

4. Katherine Bindley. "Teachers texting students: Should schools ban or encourage?" *Huffington Post*. April 17, 2012. Retrieved from www.huffingtonpost.com/2012/04/16/teachers-texting-students_n_1427418.html.

5. Staff. "Educator's guide to digital risk." *Center for Safe and Responsible Internet Use*. November 2011. Retrieved from www.embracingdigitalyouth.org/reports-issue-briefs/issue-briefs/educators-guide/.

6. Kenneth Burke. "107 texting statistics that answer all your questions." *Text Request*. January 24, 2019. Retrieved from https://www.textrequest.com/blog/texting-statistics-answer-questions/.

7. Ibid.

8. Jana Hollingsworth. "Teen callers turn to texting on Minnesota suicide hotline." *Education Week*. February 8, 2012. Retrieved from www.edweek.org/ew/articles/2012/02/08/20tech-wire.h31.html.

9. Burke, "107 texting statistics that answer all your questions."

10. Staff. "Cyberspace: Love online." *Psychology Today*. December 28, 2011. Retrieved from www.psychologytoday.com/articles/200412/cyberspace-love-online. See also Aaron Ben-Ze'Ev. *Love online: Emotions on the Internet*. 2004. New York: Cambridge University Press.

11. Yoav Gonen, "Less than friends: Teachers told, 'stay offline with students.'" *New York Post*. March 22, 2012. Retrieved from www.nypost.com/p/news/local/less_than_friends_ADEVxfo6cGZfn5zRUKxjGK#ixzz25KSOJfzE.

12. Kontji Anthony. "School investigating dirty text messages sent by teacher to student." *WMC News*. July 27, 2008. Retrieved from https://www.wmcactionnews5.com/story/8229013/school-investigating-dirty-text-messages-sent-by-teacher-to-student/.

13. Joshua Rhett Miller. "Text messages reveal how teacher allegedly lured teen student into sex." *New York Post*. December 17, 2018. Retrieved from https://nypost.com/2018/12/17/text-messages-reveal-how-teacher-allegedly-lured-teen-student-into-sex/.

14. Staff. "Oregon sex abuse case highlights teacher-student texting." *Associated Press*. March 21, 2012. Retrieved from www.kval.com/news/local/Oregon-sex-abuse-case-highlights-texting-between-teachers-students-143563016.html.

15. Darrell Smith. "Bullied 13-year-old beaten at Southern California middle school dies from his injuries." *The Sacramento Bee*. September 25, 2019. Retrieved from https://www.sacbee.com/news/california/article235484157.html.

16. Jasmine Garsd. "Should sex work be decriminalized? Some activists say it's fine." *NPR*. March 22, 2019. Retrieved from https://www.npr.org/2019/03/22/705354179/should-sex-work-be-decriminalized-some-activists-say-its-time.

17. Michelle Brandt. "Internet addiction: Too much of a good thing?" *Stanford News*. October 18, 2006. Retrieved from http://news.stanford.edu/news/2006/october18/med-internet-101806.html.

18. Ibid.

19. Staff. "Parents: Cyber-bullying led to teen's suicide." *Good Morning America*. November 19, 2011. Retrieved from http://abcnews.go.com/GMA/story?id=3882520&page=1; see also www.meganmeierfoundation.org/megansStory.php.

20. Denise Witmer. "High school survival guide for parents." *About.com*. July 6, 2012. Retrieved from http://parentingteens.about.com/od/highschool/u/highschool.htm. Cf. Staff. "The parent's guide to high school." *Education.com*. July 6, 2012. Retrieved from www.education.com/grade/high-school/.

21. R. Antrop-Gonzales and A. de Jesus. "Toward a theory of critical care in urban small school reform." 2006. *Education* 19(4): 409–33. Cf. L. K. Brendto, M. Brokenleg, and S. Van Bokern. *Reclaiming youth at risk: Our hope for the future*. 2002. Bloomington, IN: Solution Tree; cf. also Nel Noddings, *The challenge to caring in schools: An alternative approach to education*. 2005. New York: Teachers College Press.

22. Sarah D. Sparks. "Why teacher-student relationships matter." *Education Week.* March 12, 2019. Retrieved from https://www.edweek.org/ew/articles/2019/03/13/why-teacher-student-relationships-matter.html. Cf. Sara Rimm-Kaufman and Lia Sandilos. "Improving students' relationships with teachers to provide essential supports for learning." *American Psychological Association.* 2019. Retrieved from https://www.apa.org/education/k12/relationships.

23. Theo Wubbels. "Two decades of research on teacher-student relationships in class." 2005. *International Journal of Educational Research* 43(1–2): 6–24.

24. Isca Salzberger-Wittenberg, Gianna Henry, and Elsie Osborne. "The emotional experience of learning and teaching." 1984. *Journal of Child Psychotherapy* 10: 125–27.

Chapter 6

Purpose, Policy, and Protection

The building block is the moral purpose of the individual teacher. Scratch a good teacher and you will find moral purpose.

—Michael Fullan

Moral purpose is defined as a sense of commitment toward people with (1) clearly defined objective civic and character goals, (2) well-marked academic objectives and standards-aligned assessments which measure achievement, and (3) joint commitments comprising the families, schools, and communities at large—all co-authorities involved in the process. Essentially, moral purpose is larger than self[1] and contains elements of teacher-focused elements found in more traditional education.

In the last decade of the twentieth century, every American teacher heard how important his or her role was as the moral leader in the classroom. Even some European nations, which became models for the education direction in the United States, were in on the idea.[2] Scholars such as Michael Fullan viewed the teacher as the moral agent, in that he or she was considered the cornerstone of *moral purpose* in the classroom.[3] Thus, the teacher was of primary importance and the basis of education. They were told that they were the most important figures in the class. But this is no longer the case.

Whether teachers worked in English Second language, Gifted and Talented programs, Special Education, or conventional classrooms, teachers were deemed educational moral agents.[4] This was expected even of college professors in teacher education programs. That was then, but this now.

So what is the purpose of a teacher today? Is there a way to assess such a question? This question must be considered afresh, since American schools and education are very different places than they were some decades ago.

Moral purpose still exists. But a teacher's moral purpose is obscured by unresolved societal issues and the inability to gain academic traction with students. It is also made more difficult because the student is now of greater importance than his or her teacher. One reason for this is the needs of students.

Like moral purpose, moral agency can still be found in schools. However, the moral agency that is practiced is a far cry from the heavily weighted academic and assessment eras of No Child Left Behind, Race to the Top, and Common Core. Moral purpose has also shifted. It has shifted from the teacher to the institution.

Today's schools are social agencies, with children viewed much more as clients and patients rather than as academic students. Teachers are facilitators charged to meet the needs of whole children. The focus in schools has changed from student learning to empathy. This means that before students can learn properly, their personal, emotional, and physical needs must be met.

Schools have added the responsibilities of (1) assisting those with special needs, (2) offering emotional counseling and mental health care, (3) feeding children meals, and (4) training teachers to deal with everything from autism to poverty to trauma and violence. The former educational agency during the academic and assessment high-stakes eras was much more focused on cognitive education, with emphases on teachers 'teaching and learners' learning. Currently, the focus is clearly on social, emotional, and physical needs in safe-space environments.

The question must be asked as to which point of focus better prepares students for the twenty-first-century real world. In figuring out the answer, there certainly is a multitude of cultural and social distractions for both teachers and students along the way.

EDUCATION IN TRANSITION

By the year 2022, most newly trained teachers will not have any personal recollection of the twentieth century. Soon, millennials and Generation Z teachers will occupy most classrooms as teachers in America's public schools. What does this mean for the transition in the education profession? What do we know about the younger hires of today? Will their training be sufficient? What will characterize them, and can we visualize how they are likely to view relationships with students and others?

Since the twentieth-century impeachment trial of President Bill Clinton, resulting in a loss of license to practice law, the nation underwent a radical moral shift. It became commonplace for people to delineate certain behaviors and categorize their lives into private and public entities. It was as if what a person did on their private time had no impact on their public persona.

A strange phenomenon occurred in schools in many communities. Parents had to explain to their children about oral sex and how it was different from intercourse. Sex was in the air and on the air, all over the networks. It happened to be introduced by way of a president's peccadillos. Even today, teachers can still hear the justification for a certain sex act, because it somehow is not viewed as sexual intercourse. This phenomenon of compartmentalization of public and private lives is near prophetic in the words of John Dewey in 1909:

> The psychological side of education sums itself up, of course, in a consideration of character. It is a commonplace to say that the development of character is the end of all schoolwork. The difficulty lies in the execution of the idea. In addition, an underlying difficulty in this execution is the lack of a clear conception of what character means. . . .
>
> In our moral books and lectures we may lay the stress upon good intentions, etc. But we know practically that the kind of character we hope to build up through our education is one that not only has good intentions but that insists upon carrying them out. Any other character is wishy-washy; it is goody, not good. The individual must have the power to stand up and count for something in the actual conflicts of life. He must have initiative, insistence, persistence, courage, and industry. He must, in a word, have all that goes under the name "*force* of character."[5]

John Goodlad places Dewey in a more modern context when he says, "Yes, teachers require training, but they also need education, in the very best sense of the word. . . . Without this modeling, teachers of potential teachers run the danger of conveying that tiresome image, 'Do as I say; not as I do.'"[6] What could be a greater example of compartmentalization than this!

Can Teachers Control Themselves?

Teachers cross the line to begin inappropriate relationships with students for many reasons. The word *relationship* implies something much more intimate and intricate than a choice or act. If there is an assumption that teachers are desperate, in that they have little control over what they do, then the nation truly faces a national emergency beyond measure.

School districts are acutely aware of the times in which they find themselves. The hypersexual environment of hormones and students is something many teachers seem to comprehend. Yet with this understanding comes an imbalance of one's moral compass. To this end, consider the following five cases of teacher predation with three questions in mind: (1) what can districts do differently or do better at the interview stage to discover a person's underlying motivation to teach? (2) how do districts deal with teacher candidates whose worldviews demonstrate a different moral standard on certain issues?

and (3) what are the best ways to approach the delicate concerns of inappropriate teacher-student relationships and determine where teacher candidates stand, without causing offense?

- A thirty-six-year-old Strongsville High School teacher offered herself as a date in the school's Win a Date with the Teacher contest. A seventeen-year-old student won the date. Over time, the student and the teacher developed a close friendship, within which a sexual relationship began between the two. The teacher's actions were eventually discovered and she was arrested. Upon arrest, the teacher was fired and later pled guilty.[7]
- A thirty-one-year-old South Central High School teacher was convicted of taking indecent liberties with a student. The teacher was unable to explain why her cell phone records indicated that she had talked extensively to her seventeen-year-old lover, an estimated 130 times in a two-month period.[8]
- A thirty-four-year-old Culver City music teacher was charged with attempting to perform lewd acts on an eleven-year-old girl. He was arrested after he sent the girl inappropriate photographs and e-mail messages on a cell phone that he had given her for their private use.[9]
- A thirty-six-year-old lesbian teacher and coach at Lecanto High School was arrested for having a sexual relationship with a fifteen-year-old female student. The teacher was sentenced to two years of house arrest and eight years of probation. She served no jail time.[10]
- A thirty-one-year-old Buena Vista Township band teacher was charged with having sex with at least five students, one as young as fourteen.[11]

School districts must become proactive when it comes to interviewing teacher candidates. Districts must also revisit their expectations of teachers and the limits placed on their employment when it comes to their relationships with students. It is recommended that this be done twice a year, in line with professional development, required mandatory reporter updates, and other required sessions, such as those on drugs, alcohol, smoking, and vaping. In the final analysis, the concerns of inappropriate teacher-student relationships should be treated today in the same way as other age-relevant topics for students.

Proactive versus Reactive

Teachers should be required to sign off on the information, which would be best handled in formal faculty sessions. Teacher candidates should be required to acknowledge in writing that they have read and understood the teacher-student relationship guidelines, along with the mandatory reporter requirements. This set of requirements places any abuse of students by teachers reportable by law.

Students should also be instructed about the relationships they form with teachers and what boundaries districts expect students to honor. Again, taking a proactive approach with faculty and students is the safest and best way to move in the direction of safeguarding against life-altering and career-ending poor decisions.

Heightened States

America is at a point of transition, and education is not immune to this transition. People now live in a very sensually heightened and sexually explicit society. Not only are emotions at the ready but so also are sensual and sexual proclivities. The fact is that younger teachers and younger teacher candidates do not recall when pornography, adult web cam chats and shows, smartphone videos, sex sites, and immediate interpersonal communications were not readily available. The time between thoughts and actions has been shortened to seconds. This means that any notion, idea, or even temptation can be explored with a tap of an icon or the click of a mouse.

School districts may now be at the point in interviews where administrators must ask tough questions about candidates' views on sexuality, sexual relationships, use of technology in professional and private times, and any moral practices they think might spill into the classroom. In a perfect world, the answer would be yes. However, the fragmented culture in which we live has seen to it that because of political implications, public and private actions have been cordoned off from being synchronized, until an arrest occurs, that is. It is then too late.

Even so, veteran teachers might often disagree with any action that even hints at the notion of disclosure of information, which they and their teachers' association deem as private. But America's sex culture is already having serious impacts upon students. Something has to change. Predators are right there using this very privacy disagreement to their own advantage with students.

Several matters are real concerns. Years of experience as a classroom teacher are no guarantees of safety. Likewise, legislation would confirm legal interview questions to ask state-level or public government employees. The matter is open for political and contractual negotiations. Nevertheless, the safety of America's students requires the reformation of this process and doing nothing is unacceptable.

One of the downsides of cultural sexual empowerment is that it may eventually open candidates to interview questions they would rather not answer publicly. Some issue-oriented groups want to be free to proclaim their sexuality but forbid anyone from asking about the way it would play out with our nation's children.

Consider also a hypothetical male who is quite brazen in his lifestyle and flirts with female students in class and from home, using technology, even posting shirtless for photos he sends them. How can we say his actions wouldn't affect his relationships with his students? Does the school district have a right to know about his predispositions, use of technology, reputation, or whether he is seeking his first teaching job or is a veteran teacher?

Consider a few all-too-common experiences in schools today. The first situation involved several teenage girls interviewed a few years back. Conversations revealed a situation they felt was getting out of control. Their concerns involved a single, young male teacher, whom the girls said made them feel uncomfortable. The discomfort was because they believed the teacher was looking down their tops, as he walked up and down the rows. From the front of the room, the teacher was caught staring at girls' legs. The girls stated that his actions made them feel very uncomfortable.

The school's response was quite generic, placing some of the responsibility onto the students while noting and reporting their concerns exactly. The girls were then told, "Maybe if you wore clothes that didn't reveal so much cleavage or didn't wear your shorts so high, there wouldn't be a temptation to look." Sometimes teenagers are not fully aware of the way their bodies appear to others. And sometimes they are deeply aware and seek attention. Regardless, any teacher who tends to be aroused by teenage displays of their bodies is allowing inappropriate reactions to occur.

Do students sometimes dress in ways that attract adult eyes? Certainly, they do. This is a by-product of America's sex culture. Regardless of student attire, how they smell, the cuteness of their smiles, or how mature their bodies appear, teachers must not allow themselves to find pleasure in their students' physical appearance. They are children and most are legal minors.

Perhaps the time has come for stricter dress codes for our public schools. This is easier said than done. It would require an entire cultural shift in the minds of many. Frankly, if some of the visual temptation was removed from the classroom, less complaints could occur. In districts that do not train teachers about proper classroom decorum, appropriate teacher-student relationships, and behavioral boundaries, there is professional negligence at risk.

No one knows just how many teachers and students have engaged in sexual relationships over the years. There are estimates based on the reports.[12] The way things work in education is that when no incident is reported and arrest is made, no file is started. It is as if certain incidents never occurred.

Teachers have told stories about their own time in public and private schools. Some of the stories about their own instructors and affairs and rumors of relationships swirled about campuses. Many of these incidents were apparently overlooked. Times were certainly different years ago. Immoral teachers then and immoral teachers now are still immoral. Not reporting immorality and inappropriate teacher-student relationships does not negate immorality or inappropriateness.

THE IMMORAL TEACHER

One needs to look no farther than our nation's cities, in terms of how bad the problem is with sex between teachers and students. The problem is so bad in some cities that districts have actually hired teachers with immoral personal histories. For example, teachers from Boston to Chicago, Los Angeles to Dallas, and San Francisco to Atlanta have been fired when revelations of their sexual past have come to light—digital light, that is.

Some teachers appeared or even starred in several adult films. In many cases, these porn stars-turned-teachers thought nothing of keeping their pasts hidden while accepting positions to work with teenagers. But word about their past profession eventually gets out, and tech-savvy teenagers hunt down the evidence on porn sites. On more than a few occasions teenagers have discovered more about their teachers than one could ever have expected.

Aside from the prurient past of these teachers—in some cases, the very distant past—should not this discovery have been made during their application interviews? Due to the nature of some older students, holding their information over the heads of teachers for blackmail would not be beyond question. There are stories of students seeking money and sex from teachers, in exchange for a promise not to reveal anything. This begs the question, how private is private when dealing with the promises of students?

Where there is great trust, there is often increased temptation. And where there is such great temptation, there must also be much greater accountability. Should the public give *a wink and a nod* to a teacher whose past youthful recklessness might stir the raging hormones of teenagers? How many would think such a past would not be a distraction in classrooms? What if the teacher is starring in current porn films?

Films showing teachers naked, bound, and sexually abused hardly provide the kinds of images teenagers need to start their days off right or around which to shape their views of adults and sex. Students' brains have difficulty enough focusing on the tasks of the classroom. Add smart technology and videos on demand and more than a little distraction is at hand. Districts must consider not only the past experiences of those they hire but also the applicant's moonlighting work as employees of the district.

Moral compromises can become common practice, and adults who choose to engage in morally compromising behavior do not set good examples for

students. The adult's compromise becomes the teenager's justification.[13]
Though no one is perfect, a teacher who *practices* immorality as if to perfect
it is no academic mentor or moral role model. But such a teacher might be
the temptation to which a student succumbs out of his or her own weakness
or curiosity.

Administrators' Roles

Setnor-Byer, and Salcedo maintain that much of the responsibility for appropriate relationships on campus falls on the administrator. Their position is
teachers do not need to be taught that intimate relationships with minors are
illegal or even inappropriate. Such knowledge is presumed as a professional,
listed in states' codes of conduct, and are basically common sense, according
to the authors. Instead, the authors contend that administrators should focus
on the following:[14]

- Summarize the conduct that school administrators expect of all school
  personnel and the actions to be taken if suspicious behaviors are
  observed;
- Identify the behavioral signs that indicate a child is uncomfortable with a
  school employee's conduct;
- Characterize four types of behavioral triggers that create risks for school
  employees;
- List general rules of behavior that help avoid claims of misconduct;
- Recognize personality traits and motivating factors that lead to inappropriate relationships;
- Analyze actions by asking peer-observation and self-policing questions that
  help detect potentially inappropriate behaviors; and
- Describe the criminal, civil, and ethical consequences of inappropriate
  behavior.

With all due respect, an administrator cannot address the items in the
earlier list without including some commentary on relationships. America's
culture has changed drastically in the past decade. What had had been presumed as a professional is not necessarily the case any longer. How else can
someone justify working in illicit work in the evenings and then claim such
work has no bearing on what is done during the day as a teacher, while in the
classroom? While administrators might not feel comfortable about addressing
inappropriate relationships between teachers and students, they will be more
uncomfortable if they are called into court and placed on a witness stand during a trial alleging his or her negligence.

PROFESSIONAL CONDUCT FOR TEACHERS

States develop education principles of ethics and professional codes of conduct for teachers. Both of these apply to veterans and new hires, alike. Districts are also developing acceptable-use policies for teachers' use of technology. In many cases, the statements are "commandments" in the negative, specifying what teachers may *not* do.

Five states' policies regarding teacher conduct with students are presented later, followed by a brief analysis of two of these states: Texas and Alabama.

Various regions of the nation are represented in Alabama,[15] California,[16] Illinois,[17] New York,[18] and Texas.[19] Table 6.1 is a summary of the data collected from five states' Department of Education websites, pertaining to

Table 6.1   Five State Excerpts Pertaining to Teacher-Student Relationships

State	Statement
Alabama	**Standard 4: Teacher-Student Relationship** Unethical conduct includes but is not limited to 1. committing any act of child abuse; 2. committing or soliciting any unlawful sex act; and 3. soliciting, encouraging, or consummating an inappropriate written, verbal, or physical relationship with a student.
California	The state of California does not have a state-level teacher-student relationship code prohibition, and it does not require schools to have policies that lay out clear boundaries between teachers and students. Some districts have taken it upon themselves to draft codes of ethics due to litigation. The California Teachers Association (CTA) has laid out its expectations for its association members.
Illinois	**Principle 1: Responsibility to Students** 1. Respect inherent dignity and worth of each student by assuring that learning environment reflects respect and equal opportunity. 2. Maintain a professional relationship with students at all times.
New York	**New York State Code of Ethics for Educators** **(Principles 1 and 2)** 1. Educators nurture the intellectual, physical, emotional, social, and civic potential of each student. 2. Teachers respect the inherent dignity and worth of each student. 3. Educators are role models, displaying the habits of mind and work necessary to develop and apply knowledge.
Texas	**Ethical Conduct toward Students (Standards 3.6 and 3.8)** 3.6: The educator shall not solicit or engage in sexual conduct or a romantic relationship with a student or a minor. 3.8: The educator shall maintain appropriate professional educator-student relationships and boundaries based on a reasonably prudent educator standard.

language regarding teacher ethics, expectations of teacher conduct, and statements addressing teacher-student relationships.

Although each state is different in its expectations and expressions, there are a few common threads of which to take note. Three common threads include:

- professionalism in action and relationships with all stakeholders,
- making certain to demonstrate respect to colleagues, students, and families, and
- and a focus on intellectual pursuits and the well-being of students.

States have published professional codes of conduct for teachers. But some of these codes apply less than clear and concise policy language. The documentation is posted on their state's Department of Education websites. The codes reviewed indicate the directions many states are heading. Since states are seeing alarming increases in inappropriate teacher-student relationships, this fact alone should prompt every state to move quickly. Rather than focusing on the punitive, some states posit expectations for their teachers.

For example, Texas, "during fiscal 2017–18 . . . opened 429 cases into inappropriate student-educator relationships, an approximate 42 percent increase from the prior year"[20] of 2016–2017. Some attributed the rise in reporting to the #MeToo movement. The "number of teachers flagged statewide for having sex and other inappropriate relationships with students continues to rise, according to the Texas Education Agency."[21] Under Texas' SB7, "Teachers can be charged with an improper relationship with a student regardless of whether or not the student is in their district."[22] Texas legislators are also exploring whether or not to develop a "do not hire list,"[23] which would also be available to private schools to determine the backgrounds and records of those seeking employment.

In the city of San Antonio, by itself, there is a disturbing trend of cases of alleging teacher-student sex. Teachers were forced either to give up their licenses to teach or their licenses were revoked. Unfortunately, from Alabama to Texas or New York to California, or Washington, every state in America is dealing with these types of crimes and outcomes. Table 6.2 lists several school districts in the San Antonio area and the outcomes of the allegations as reported up to 2017.

Another example is the state of Alabama. Since 2010, inappropriate sexual relationships between teachers and students in Alabama exceeded 200 cases annually. Alabama has one of the "highest rates of inappropriate teacher-student sexual relationships."[24] In response to this, Alabama has "criminalized teacher-student sexual relationships."[25] The state has developed training for its teachers on what types of relationships are proper and which ones are not.

Table 6.2 Texas Teacher License Revocations and Filed Criminal Charges: San Antonio

Independent School Districts	Number of San Antonio Area Teaching Licenses Revoked	Number of San Antonio Area Teachers Charged with a Crime
Northside	20	4
San Antonio	17	6
North East	10	2
Comal	6	2
Southwest	4	2
Judson	4	1
South San Antonio	3	1
Harlandale Independent School District	2	0
Edgewood	2	1
Southside	2	1
New Braunfels	2	1
Comfort	2	1
Alamo Heights	1	0
Boerne	1	0
Seguin	1	0
Schertz-Cibolo-Universal City	1	0
Marion Independent	1	0
Totals	79	22

One of its educator ethics modules deals specifically with the issue of boundary violations.[26]

One would think that states could work with unions and teachers associations to reform the interview process. But student safety has less precedence over politics and the union protection of teachers. Some things are obviously being missed in the process and what is missed, in some cases, leads to heartache down the road for many students, parents, and education stakeholders.

INTERVIEWING TEACHER CANDIDATES

Some states' professional codes of conduct and education policies are now reflecting the attention of the seriousness of background checks and vetting of teacher candidates. However, when pushed to take action, school districts would rather pass the trash than become involved in expensive lawsuits for privacy violations.

Another reason districts are slow to act is the enormous teacher shortage facing so many cities and states. Districts are wrestling with balancing whether to maintain the normal credentialing process or speed up placement of new teachers to alleviate shortages. In the process, the risks increase under pressure to provide staffing statewide.

States that have convoluted codes for teachers need to either rewrite or revise their teacher-student relationships guidelines. The next step is to make certain these find their way into the hiring process without cutting corners. The importance of the interview and screening process is paramount as a first step to putting student safety first.

Changes in the Teacher-Candidate Interview Process

How does anyone recognize a bad teacher applicant in interview or on paper—especially if the teacher applicant is new and has glowing references from professors? Résumés are padded, references may be biased, yet somehow there must be a determination as to whether the person sitting opposite the interviewers is both qualified to work with students and worth the risk. Professional hiring determinations often occur after several personal interviews. Does anyone clearly know whether someone is at greater risk for engaging in inappropriate relationships with students? Might there be signs?

With the ubiquity of communication technologies, and the prevalence of sexual explicitness in our culture, interviewees' questions must be approached differently. A good start is to perform a comprehensive and extensive online search on each teacher candidate. This means more than a background check and fingerprinting. Such a process requires more than a cursory approach to screening. It actually would require a hard look into the various webs for information.

The pressure to fill vacant teaching positions is real, and as a result teacher placement is sometimes quicker and riskier than it should be. The rationale is that having credentialed adults in classrooms is preferred over not having them. Some larger districts assume the risks of placing *warm, breathing bodies* in rooms with teenagers without having gone through an extensive and protective series of checks. The trend of nontraditional teacher training and alternative certification pathways is adding to the concerns of proper screening.[27] But schools that have difficulty finding teachers are less apt to spend the requisite time in interview process.

Reform must occur in the interviewing process of teacher candidates. As a parallel reform, it must also consider how best to incentivize people to enter the career of education in the first place. Questions about moral purpose and moral practices and their impacts upon education, in general, should be raised during interviews.

Laws must change to better protect students and families. Predators, and those who might desire sex with our students, take advantage of policy loopholes. Hopeful crossing of fingers is not acceptable policy. Schools must hire teachers with clear moral purposes and must ask candidates to define this purpose, both in words and potential actions in the classroom.

States must require moral purposes to be addressed in their teacher training courses, especially as it pertains to educational philosophy and teaching practices and instructional methods. Education is not a perfect world. However, reducing the imperfection minimizes risks and demonstrates a priority of protecting students in America's sex-saturated culture.

AMERICA'S SEX CULTURE AND THE TEACHER CANDIDATE INTERVIEW

The following questions are controversial and, in most cases, would not appear as part of a formal job interview, as the process stands today. But these questions should be in the backs of the minds of the interviewers, with each prospective teacher candidate.

- How important is knowledge of an interviewee's sexual identity or claim of gender?
- How controversial and distracting would a transgender or transsexual teacher be for a district?
- What restrictions are there to asking questions about an applicant's open sexual lifestyle, once the person states he or she has *come out* and is *openly* living as such?
- May districts query teacher applicants regarding their uses of technology?
- Are teachers' past online postings fair game?
- Should interviewers know whether teacher candidates have ever belonged to organizations or websites that promote bigotry, anticommunity activism, or violent behaviors?

Districts do have the obligation to determine whether the teachers they hire may sully the reputation of the district. Nevertheless, they are heavily constrained from delving too deeply into politically protected groups' backgrounds and practices. There are so many questions, and the answers to these questions are as varied as there are needs for school districts.

What Are the Fears?

Issues stemming from teachers' unions, violations of personal and state privacy laws, and fears of resource-draining lawsuits might very well keep districts from asking any tough questions. Americans live at a time when sex and social media are in the cultural mainstream. These have changed many cultural rules of the past. We live in a new age of sexuality that has not been kind to educational moral purpose and has ensnared teachers and students in communities all across the nation.

The time is right for school districts to bring lawyers into the interview process, along with experts on child abuse and adolescent psychologists. Their input would be valuable in the interview process. Laws should change to make certain to allow additional professionals to offer their opinions on teacher candidates before offering employment.

Teacher applicants should be asked to open their social media postings to the interviewers. Online behaviors are sometimes very different from one's regular, daily life. What an interviewee might have intended to keep secret could find its way onto a public forum, causing serious legal issues and community embarrassment. Opening personal websites should become part of a background check, just like fingerprinting, for transferring teachers to different schools, both inside and outside the districts to which they apply to work with children.

TEACHER CANDIDATE INTERVIEW QUESTIONS AND RATIONALES

The following list of seven questions comprises what some teachers and potential teachers might consider a bit more personal than necessary. However, after checking with local law enforcement, consulting personal and professional opinions of attorney friends, and reading interview procedures from other professions, the consensus is clear. On this issue there is agreement that more aggressive protective measures are necessary, over and against outcries of privacy invasions. Few parents would ever argue against this policy and practice. However, few have the political will to legislate the consensus.

The teacher interview questions suggested in the following section would be used for new hires to districts. Veteran educators who are also newly hired by different districts or have transferred a credential to a different state should also be subject to this scrutiny. The list includes select questions that should be part of either the oral or the written interview stages for new hires.

Interview Question #1: Divorce

Interviewers should ask about information provided to them on the written application. For example, "We notice that you have checked that you are divorced. Have you been divorced more than once, and how recent is/are the divorce(s)? Would you mind providing a few details as to whether any form of physical, sexual, or substance abuse was involved?"

Rationale for Asking Question #1

Teacher applicants check the box indicating marital status, and this is on state and federal tax returns and on social security and salary deduction paperwork. Asking about divorce is appropriate, especially if the interviewee's significant recent relationships with adults have been violent or abusive as that might affect the classroom or student learning. Students will ask about teacher's relationships. Divorce is commonplace today, but the reasons for the divorce could affect the classroom environment adversely, as well as the relationships with the faculty, particularly among close friends.

Interview Question #2: Drugs

Applicants should be queried about their views on, and personal use of, drugs, whether recreational or prescribed. They should be asked to address how teachers on such substances could add to or diminish teacher performance and student learning. Moving toward taking a drug test for all teaching candidates would be a plus and reduce the risks of teacher applicants with drug problems.

Rationale for Asking Question #2

Districts that have policies about tobacco and alcohol use—as well as vaping on campus—often do not have policies about teachers participating in recreational drugs. It has also been taboo to ask about prescribed or illegal drugs and prescription drugs can also negatively affect a teacher's performance.

Teachers' support for legalizing current illegal substances does affect the mindsets of students, especially those seeking personal justification for alternate or nontraditional cultural practices. Districts risk much by placing a teacher when the candidate is known to use prescription drugs, marijuana, or any illegal substances recreationally. Interviewers must be able to query teacher candidates: "I see you checked that you have no drug offenses in the past. Is this accurate? Please elaborate."

Interview Question #3: Tattoos and Piercings

Applicants should not be barred because of body art. Yet the question is appropriate given the culture in which we live. A good question to ask is, "Do you have any tattoos or piercings that would be uncovered throughout the course of the regular school day?"

Rationale for Asking Question #3

The shift in culture has seen a marked increase of people adorning themselves with body art, piercings, and/or tattoos. If a teacher has an offensive tattoo and there is any chance teenagers will see it, then the district could be liable for negligence, particularly if a student, teacher, or parent is triggered by the perception of an offensive symbol or phrase.

For example, if during the interview process a teacher withheld past or present gang affiliation, or if students later saw a Nazi symbol tattooed on the teacher, the community would be very angry. Self-mutilation, ear plugging, brow piercing, tongue studs, and cheek and nose piercings are still in style for some. Districts must consider the extent these adornments, including quasi-mutilations, affect the educational process or distract from student learning.

Interview Question #4: Adult-Film Industry

This question bears directly on the topic of this book. Interviewers should have queries such as these on the written application, so as to prompt discussion, if necessary. Past involvement in an illicit industry should not necessarily rule out a person from employment. That aside, possible questions could be, "Is there anything in your past or present that connects you either through direct or indirect activity, or through profit to (1) the adult film industry, (2) the adult sex-toy industry, (3) online pornography (either the appearance in or purchase or sale of these materials), (4) hosting or maintaining an adult or erotic website, or (5) the signing of any past or present contract to associate you in any way with the adult sex industry?"

Rationale for Asking Question #4

Stating the obvious is sometimes necessary. The argument that personal practice on one's own time, outside of work, has no effect on the performance of the teacher on the job is myopic and outdated. The effects on students and the community, once they find out about the split-lives of teachers, are significant. In fact, they are life-altering in some cases, especially if students were involved personally.

Students require good mentoring as their bodies and minds mature. Sexuality remains something that is deeply personal and should not be flaunted, made light of, or impersonalized and objectified as recreational. For example, teenagers preparing for relationships as adults need mentoring to make good choices, including information that counters the philosophy that casual sex is inconsequential. Despite what America's sex culture proclaims, teenagers having sex *is* consequential.

Interview Question #5: Sexual Abuse

Domestic abuse is a major problem in the United States. Part of this abuse is sexual. The recent cases of Weinstein and Epstein are examples of sexual abuse. Applicants should be asked their opinions about (1) how they would handle victims of child sexual abuse in their classes, (2) whether teachers sexually abused as children pose a higher risk of abusing one or more children today.

Rationale for Asking Question #5

Teachers who are arrested for sex crimes with their students often claim their past child sexual abuse as part of the reason for their crimes. Given that statistics and testimony indicate that there is a greater likelihood that adults who commit sexual crimes with students have suffered child sexual abuse themselves, it would be prudent during the interview process to discover whether psychologically impacting crimes were committed against the teacher candidate. Interviewers must consider the balance between rights and legality, with negligence and the risks to student safety. If states are serious about *whole child education*, then nothing works harder against this philosophy like not supporting safer policies and procedures to safeguard the whole child.

Interview Question #6: Addictions

Interviewers should know whether a person they intend to hire has any addictions. They might ask, "Are you aware of any addictions you have to legal or illegal substances, the Internet, or personal behaviors that would predispose you to moral weaknesses in front of children and colleagues?" This question is similar to question number two. The intent is to focus down on the rampant problem in America and determine whether a teacher candidate is part of the problem or intends to become part of a solution.

Rationale for Asking Question #6

Tobacco use and smoking are generally considered addictions and are harmful. They are not allowed on campuses anywhere. Districts have policies and states have laws about purchasing smoking and chewing materials.

The newest addiction, which has medical professional concerns, is *vaping*. Students as young as elementary age are showing signs of addiction and vapers are beginning to come down with unexplained respiratory illnesses.[28] A few vapers have even died from the practice. Districts should know the daily vices of the candidates they intend to hire, as these will eventually come to the forefront and possibly inhibit teacher performance and attendance.

Alcohol problems, drug addictions, smoking, chewing, vaping, and other vices are problems today for adults and children. It is fair to ask hypothetical questions about how a potential teacher candidate would deal with a district's substance-free environment.

Everyone accepts that smokers must extinguish their cigarettes from the moment they set foot on campus. It is equally fair to ask in what ways certain addictions might inhibit a person's ability to be effective in the classroom. Some of these include (1) daily use of prescribed pain medications, (2) habitual use of tobacco products, (3) vaping, as well as things like (4) pornography and sex addictions.

Interview Question #7: Online Media

The Internet is so much a part of many of our lives that it is time to embed questions about usage in teacher candidate interviews. For example, "What is your current use of online social media sites, and what are some examples of private sites to which you subscribe? Would you have any problem disabling or deleting these sites before any offer to hire you are extended? Would you have an issue with allowing a neutral third-party access to your social media accounts and view your pages, as a prerequisite to being hired?"

Rationale for Asking Question #7

Teachers must be extra careful about what they post online individually and with the groups with which they associate. Being careful and being accountable are packaged under different expectations for the teacher. The former relies on the honor system, where the district would accept the word of the teacher. The latter would be more along the lines of the example provided by many law-enforcement agencies and political agencies that vet those whom they seek to hire. Which of these is more acceptable for school districts?

TEACHERS' RIGHTS VERSUS STUDENTS' PROTECTIONS

In recent history, the California state legislature voted down SB1530, a bill written by a state Democratic senator that would have made it easier for school districts to fire teachers accused of gross misconduct. The bill emerged partly in reaction to a Miramonte Elementary School teacher who was accused of lewd acts with his students, including spoon-feeding his semen to students and lacing vanilla cookies with the same.[29]

Hundreds of cell phone photos were seized after the arrest of sixty-one-year-old third-grade teacher Mark Berndt. Along with another teacher at the school, Berndt was accused of committing lewd acts upon children. Berndt pleaded not guilty to twenty-three counts of lewdness on a child. Over ninety combined teachers and school administrators at the elementary school were released from their jobs and all new staffing hired after news of the scandal broke.

The California legislation was voted down in large part because the CTA and other unions that weighed-in, fearing that the legislation would harm teachers' due-process rights if districts were more easily allowed to outright fire faculty for gross misconduct. The bill did not even make it out of the California Education Committee of the state assembly.[30]

The term *gross misconduct* could have been refined clearly and carefully and the bill passed without unduly impacting teachers' rights. However, the CTA chose to defend its members' due-process rights over the children and families it serves. The inability of the CTA to see the merits of the bill is an example where sexual misconduct of a teacher is placed over student safety and political policy placed over people.

One has to wonder whether the actions of former teacher Brittni Colleps, age twenty-eight, would have been considered gross misconduct. Colleps allegedly had group sex with five male students. One of the students video-taped one of the sexual encounters, which was played in court to convict the former English teacher and mother of three children. Police examined cell phone records of one of the students and found that Colleps wrote him hundreds of text messages. On several occasions she had texted that she craved the young male and that he "had something she wanted."[31]

Then there is this case from the author's high-school alma mater. Leo Donaldson, former teacher and track coach, "exploited his position in order to engage in improper sexual contact"[32] with teenage student-athletes. Donaldson was convicted and sent to prison for seven years after "pleading guilty to aggravated sexual assault, sexual assault, endangering the welfare of a [male] child, and official misconduct."[33] As evidence that the system protects teachers over students, the victim is suing Bloomfield High School, three administrators of the school, and the Bloomfield, New Jersey Board of Education. The victim is claiming he was "improperly removed"[34] from school prior to graduation, "instead of protecting him from the predatory educator."[35]

How many teachers will be allowed to commit multiple crimes before a common-sense approach to reform addresses teacher hiring and firing practices? Do we have to continue to wait until more children are hurt, or can professionals catch some of these predispositions and errant moral compasses before they show up in the classroom? Again, a tougher process during the interview may result in safer environments.

Common-Sense Safeguards

In closing, it is entirely possible to lose sight of common sense over the clamoring of culture and the issues of education. Barbara Murray and Kenneth Murray offer sage advice for teachers, old and new.[36] Their advice is summarized in the following:

1. Remember who the adult is and do not blur this line.
2. Be careful about touching. The less touching, the better.
3. If there is an off-campus meeting, a party, or a get-together for students and the younger teacher is invited, it is best to decline.
4. When performing school-related activities when the teacher can anticipate being alone with one or more students, other adults should be invited into the activity. This accountability is very important and protects everyone involved.
5. Take extra care to guard one's private life away from school, which means taking extra precautions when posting on social media websites and when interacting personally with colleagues, students, and parents.

These are common-sense safeguards for teachers across any grade level or at any school—the kinds that do not leave students and their safety out of the equation.

SUMMARY

Moral purpose is born of (1) clearly defined objective civic and character goals, (2) well-marked academic objectives and standards-aligned assessments to measure achievement, and (3) joint commitments by the families, communities, and schools. Essentially, moral purpose is larger than self.

The teacher candidate interview process needs to be reformed. Many teachers need current, qualitative professional-development advice regarding ways to interact and relate to Generation Z students. Administrators should receive training on how to create moral accountability for faculty and staff. This training could occur at two levels: (1) teacher-training institutions and (2) regular district-level professional development.

States are slowly reforming education codes of ethics and professional principles of conduct for teachers. These codes apply to both veterans and new hires. Districts now have acceptable technology-use policies built in to their ethics statements. Some of the common threads found in states codes for teacher conduct presented include (1) professionalism, (2) making certain to respect colleagues, students, and families, and (3) focusing on intellectual pursuits.

The probing of a teacher's background or views on particular personal issues is a sensitive subject. Application and personal interview questions are suggested in the chapter, along with rationales for asking them. This chapter closes with five common-sense safeguards for teachers as they deal with navigating twenty-first-century public school classrooms and combating and working around America's sex culture.

DISCUSSION QUESTIONS

1. How would you define *moral purpose*? Explain the extent to which it is important in education.
2. What specific factors contribute to teachers and students becoming involved in inappropriate teacher-student relationships?
3. How would you identify the similarities and differences between states' professional codes of conduct, and can you suggest any changes?
4. Should interviewers and administrators have more latitude to ask personal, probing questions at new teacher candidate interviews? Why, or why not?
5. In light of the arrests of teachers accused of sex crimes with teenage students, would you add anything to the interviewing or evaluative process for the sake of student security? If so, what would you suggest?
6. In terms of the issues addressed in this chapter, what is your opinion on the balance between teachers' rights, teachers' unions, and students' rights for safety and protection?
7. How much responsibility do you think seventeen- or eighteen-year-old students should bear if they become involved in sexual relationships with any of their teachers?
8. Is there a need for professional development for teachers or a need for parent-information evenings for families in order to review (1) general academic and/or communication technologies and (2) district and school communications acceptable-use policies?
9. Has the time come to revise teacher-student sex laws and view consent of students seventeen and older as legal to engage in emotional, physical, or sexual affairs with teachers? Why, or why not?

NOTES

1. Ernest J. Zarra, III. "Character education: An analysis of state history – social science and English-language-arts curriculum frameworks and content standards." Doctoral dissertation. 1999. *University of Southern California*, p. 59. Cf. Ernest

J. Zarra, III. "Pinning down character education." Summer 2000. *Kappa Delta Pi Record* 36(4): 154–157.

2. Trygve Bergem. "The teacher as moral agent." May 1990. *Journal of Moral Education* 19(2): 88–100. Retrieved from https://eric.ed.gov/?id=EJ423793.

3. Michael Fullan. *Change forces: Probing the depths of education reform.* 1993. London, UK: The Falmer Press.

4. Bill Johnston, Andrea Juhasz, James Marken, et al. "Research in the teaching of English." May 1998. *National Council of Teachers of English* 32(2): 161–81. Retrieved from https://www.jstor.org/stable/i40004745.

5. John Dewey. *Moral principles in education.* 1909. New York: Houghton Mifflin Company, pp. 49–50. Retrieved from www.gutenberg.org/files/25172/25172-h/25172-h.htm.

6. John I. Goodlad. *Educational renewal.* 1994. San Francisco, CA: Jossey-Bass, Inc., Publishers, p. 11. Cf. Karen Lea. "Modeling: Essential for learning." *Edutopia.* March 20, 2013. Retrieved from https://www.edutopia.org/blog/modeling-essential-for-learning-karen-lea.

7. Christine Scarlett. "Her boy toy and their boy." *Today in the USA.* May 14, 2007. Retrieved from http://todayintheusa.com/page/115/?s=f%C3%A2.

8. Erin Rickert. "Jurors decide against teacher." *The Daily Reflector.* June 24, 2006. Retrieved from www.williamslawonline.com/Press-Room/Teacher_Found_Not_Guilty_of_Sex_Offense_January_24-_2006.pdf.

9. Staff. "Music teacher accused of trying to arrange sex date with girl." *Los Angeles Times.* September 19, 2011. Retrieved from http://latimesblogs.latimes.com/lanow/2011/09/music-teacher-arrested-for-attempted-lewd-act-on-child.html.

10. Staff. "Lesbian teacher rapist off hook – no jail time." *World Net Daily.* January 20, 2006. Retrieved from www.wnd.com/2006/01/34415/.

11. Staff. "Sexy substitute teacher 'has relations with boy.'" *World Net Daily.* January 25, 2006. Retrieved from http://www.freerepublic.com/focus/f-chat/1565126/posts?page=21.

12. Brian Palmer. "How many kids are sexually abused by their teachers? Probably millions." *Slate.com.* February 8, 2012. Retrieved from www.slate.com/articles/news_and_politics/explainer/2012/02/is_sexual_abuse_in_schools_very_common_.html.

13. Kip Michalak, "St. Louis Teacher fired for her adult films," *WTSP News.* March 9, 2011, accessed June 7, 2012, https://www.wtsp.com/article/home/st-louis-teacher-fired-for-her-adult-films/67-387890073; cf. Shawn McGinnis and Kennedy Ryan. "Teacher with porn past loses bid to get job back." *KTLA News.* January 16, 2013. Retrieved from https://ktla.com/2013/01/16/teacher-with-porn-past-loses-bid-to-get-job-back/; Brhe Berry and Shelley Childers. "Substitute teacher fired for filming porn in classroom: School." *ABC News.* June 25, 2019. Retrieved from https://abc13.com/substitute-teacher-fired-for-filming-porn-in-classroom-school/5363696/.

14. Anita Setnor-Byer and Martin Salcedo. "Student-teacher relationships: Where to draw the lines." *Human Equation.* May 18, 2007. Retrieved from www.thehumanequation.com/en/news_rss/articles/2007/05_18_Teacher_Student_Relationships.aspx.

15. Staff. "Alabama educator code of ethics." *Alabama Department of Education*. Retrieved from http://etico.iiep.unesco.org/sites/default/files/usa_alabama.pdf.

16. Kayla Jimenez. "School districts that don't have policies on teacher-student boundaries are paying the price." *Voice of San Diego*. June 24, 2019. Retrieved from https://www.kpbs.org/news/2019/jun/24/school-districts-dont-have-policies-teacher-studen/. Cf. Staff. "Code of ethics." *California Teachers Association*. 2019. Retrieved from https://www.cta.org/About-CTA/Who-We-Are/Code-of-Ethics.aspx.

17. Staff. "Illinois educator code of ethics." *Illinois Educator Code of Ethics Advisory Group*. n.d. Retrieved from http://www.myinfinitec.org/documents/10156/6c7bc292-77e5-48b0-9058-f7c385ffc73a.

18. Staff. "New York state code of ethics for educators." *New York State Professional Standards and Practices Board for Teaching*. Retrieved from http://www.highered.nysed.gov/tcert/pdf/codeofethics.pdf. Cf. David W. Chen. "Social media rules limit New York student-teacher contact." *New York Times*. May 2, 2012. Retrieved from www.nytimes.com/2012/05/02/nyregion/social-media-rules-for-nyc-school-staff-limits-contact-with-students.html?_r=1&pagewanted=all.

19. Staff. "Code of ethics and standard practices for Texas educators." *Texas Educator Code of Ethics and Standards*. n.d. Retrieved from https://uteach.utexas.edu/sites/default/files/files/Code_of_Ethics_and_Standard%20UPDATE.pdf.

20. Nanette Light. "Cases of improper student-teacher relationships on the rise after passage of state law cracks down on educator misconduct." *The Dallas Morning News*. November 28, 2018. Retrieved from https://www.dallasnews.com/news/education/2018/11/29/cases-of-improper-student-teacher-relationships-on-the-rise-after-passage-of-state-law-cracks-down-on-educator-misconduct/.

21. Ibid.

22. Ibid.

23. Ibid.

24. Andy. Campbell. "Alabama has highest rate of teacher-student sex abuse: Study." *Huffington Post*. December 6, 2017. Retrieved from https://www.huffpost.com/entry/alabama-highest-rate-teacher-sex_n_6479822.

25. Rachel Blidner. "Alabama teachers have more sex with students more frequently: Study." *New York Daily News*. January 15, 2015. Retrieved from https://www.nydailynews.com/news/crime/alabama-highest-rate-teacher-student-sex-study-article-1.2078895.

26. Staff. "Professional conduct and boundaries for Alabama schools." *Alabama Department of Education*. 2018. Retrieved from https://www.alsde.edu/sec/comm/General%20Counsel%20%20Legislative/PowerPoint%20-%20AL-Module%201_Teacher_Student%20Boundaries-revised.pptx.

27. Ernest J. Zarra, III. *The age of teacher shortages: Reasons, responsibilities, reactions*. 2019. Lanham, MD: Rowman & Littlefield Publishers.

28. Lucas Combos. "New vaping-linked lung injuries confirmed in King County." *Gig Harbor Patch*. October 16, 2019. Retrieved from https://patch.com/washington/gigharbor/s/gvp7m/new-vaping-linked-lung-injuries-confirmed-in-king-county?utm_term=article-slot-3&utm_source=newsletter-daily&utm_medium=email&utm_campaign=newsletter&fbclid=IwAR2eTSkCXNq5bHlrPqYbQMJU

KEv-rtJ-HtwbrImNby54DdxlNQX8d9aOvIQ. Cf. Lucas Combos. "State outlines new rules for Washington vape shops." *Gig Harbor Patch.* October 11, 2019. Retrieved from https://patch.com/washington/gigharbor/s/gvj0y/state-outlines-new-rules-for-washington-vape-shops?utm_term=article-slot-1&utm_source=newsletter-daily&utm_medium=email&utm_campaign=newsletter&fbclid=IwAR12GtEZ60cHnFSaIFjkpg5lDXsFek9k6K6XWvmuWcLwAgdM8bqnFKeSK0g.

29. Mark Duell. "I'm 'very happy you're my student': Chilling letters sent to children by 'pervert' teacher at L.A. sex scandal school." *Daily Mail.* February 10, 2012. Retrieved from www.dailymail.co.uk/news/article-2098811/Shocking-photo-Mark-Berndt-posing-tights-Mickey-Mouse-ears.html#ixzz22G54YYXt.

30. Staff. "Bill responding to la-area teacher sex case fails in assembly panel." *Bakersfield Californian.* June 28, 2012, p. 45.

31. Staff. "Texas jury sees video of teacher allegedly having sex with 4 students." *Fox News.* August 15, 2012. Retrieved from www.foxnews.com/us/2012/08/15/texas-jury-sees-video-teacher-allegedly-having-sex-with-4-students/#ixzz23iKTqrBS.

32. Craig McCarthy and Natalie Mesumeci. "New Jersey 'improperly removed' molestation victim: Suit." *New York Post.* October 16, 2019. Retrieved from https://nypost.com/2019/10/16/new-jersey-school-improperly-removed-molestation-victim-suit/?fbclid=IwAR1KSRkVRFyWSqfdB5GyyHuMx05EZSEBZpOwIQ5pPPr-NZ9A4hkRweHBss8.

33. Ibid.

34. Ibid.

35. Ibid.

36. Barbara Murray and Kenneth Murray. *Pitfalls and potholes: A checklist for avoiding common mistakes of beginning teachers.* 2004. Washington, D.C.: National Education Association.

Index

About the Author

Ernest J. Zarra, III, PhD, is a retired assistant professor of Teacher Education at Lewis-Clark State College. Zarra has five earned degrees and holds the PhD from the University of Southern California, in teaching and learning theory, with cognates in psychology and technology. He is a former Christian College First Team All-American soccer player, former teacher of the year for a prestigious California public school, and was awarded the top student in graduate education from the California State University at Bakersfield, California.

Dr. Zarra has written twelve books and more than a dozen journal articles, has designed professional development programs. He is a national conference presenter, former district professional development leader, adjunct university instructor, and a member of several national honor societies. He also participated as a speaker of the Idaho Speakers Bureau, as well as a presenter in the Lewis-Clark Presents program, bringing special topics to high-school students.

Originally from New Jersey, he and his wife Suzi, a retired California public school teacher, live in Washington State and enjoy spending time with family, which includes their first grandchild.